D0251909

PERSONALIZE YOUR FIELD GUIDE

NAME.

ADDRESS:

DATE OF BIRTH:

SOCIAL SECURITY/INSURANCE NUMBER:

EMILY HORNE &
TIM MALY

THE
INSPECTION
HOUSE

AN IMPERTINENT FIELD GUIDE
TO MODERN SURVEILLANCE

COACH HOUSE BOOKS, TORONTO

Published with the generous assistance of the Canada Council for the Arts and the Ontario Arts Council. Coach House Books also gratefully acknowledges the support of the Government of Canada through the Canada Book Fund and the Government of Ontario through the Ontario Book Publishing Tax Credit.

LIBRARY AND ARCHIVES CANADA CATALOGUING IN PUBLICATION

Horne, Emily, 1979-, author
    The inspection house : an impertinent field guide to modern surveillance / Emily Horne and Tim Maly.

(Exploded views)
Issued in print and electronic formats.
isbn 978-1-55245-301-8 (pbk.).

    1. Electronic surveillance. 2. Social control. 3. State, The.
4. Privacy, Right of. I. Maly, Tim, 1978-, author II. Title.
III. Series: Exploded views

JC596.H67 2014   323.44'82   C2014-904401-1

The Inspection House is available as an ebook: ISBN 978 1 77056 389 6.

Contents

To Whom It Ought to Concern,

This is a field guide to the rich terrain of the panopticon. Can you correctly identify a panopticon? Knowing more about surveillance enhances our experience and helps us to share encounters with friends and family.

Getting Started

Who's watching you? Make a list of all the people or institutions that are tracking you. Are you being observed directly? Are there CCTV cameras in your neighbourhood? Are your whereabouts and purchases being logged by your phone provider? Do you use a computer to access the internet? Are you carrying any credit cards or smart cards? Did you have to fill out a time sheet or report to a supervisor today? Did you hand in any assignments? Have you interacted recently with the police or emergency services personnel? Does your country conduct domestic surveillance operations? Do any other countries on your planet conduct foreign surveillance operations? Do you have friends or family who wonder where you are? Has your region been mapped? Do you ever pay bills or taxes? Do you use local utilities? Do you have any subscriptions? Do you have a to-do list? Do you track your fitness or diet goals?

Can you watch back? Once you have completed the activity, go back over the list and mark which of those agents you can observe in return. Can they see more about you, or can you see more about them? Is there anyone you can talk to about your experience of being watched?

About This Book

A field guide is a book designed to help the reader identify wildlife, architecture or other objects and networks of natural or human occurrence. It is designed to be brought into the 'field' or local area, where such objects and networks exist to help the reader distinguish between similar objects and networks.

In general, serious and scientific field identification books feature keys to assist with identification. This book does not include identification keys. Nor does it include drawings or paintings to assist the reader with a visual inspection. A visual inspection is hardly the point. This is a field guide to a conceptual terrain.

About This Terrain

The world is webbed in vast physical and virtual networks. The world has always been webbed in networks, but the latest networks are particularly vast and particularly fast.

Telecommunications and electronics (now cheap, thanks to robust global logistical networks) have mixed with business needs and an atmosphere of fear around real and imagined threats from activist, criminal and terrorist organizations (illicit networks) to encourage the implementation of sprawling surveillance networks. A significant proportion of the population regularly carry devices that, as a matter of regular operation, log their locations and activities. An even greater proportion conduct their daily affairs across a network of services that also log everything as a matter of course.

When people reach for a metaphor to understand our present condition, many grab hold of the panopticon. Often, their usage doesn't go much deeper than the meaning of the word (in Greek, *pan* meaning *all*, *optikon* meaning *seeing*). This book will help you explore further.

The Inspection House has three central players, none of which are human. The first is a collection of letters written by British philosopher Jeremy Bentham, describing his initial design of the Panopticon. The second is *Discipline & Punish*, a book written by Michel Foucault that reinterprets Bentham's Panopticon as an emblem for a particular way of organizing society. The third is our strange present condition. We will use each of these characters to try to understand the other two.

Following in the footsteps of our first two players, this book is architectural, though it contains very little architecture. Both Bentham and Foucault treat buildings as machines for disciplining, tools for altering behaviour. Their descriptions tend to be idealized or vague. We have chosen specific sites to illustrate the messy interface between power and history. Yesterday's ideologies are frozen into today's architecture. Today's ideologies must contend with or replace that inherited built environment.

How to Use This Book

The structure of the book is: seven longer chapters, each focused on a particular site and organized in a way that loosely mirrors the argument of *Discipline & Punish*. Within and between the chapters are enriching asides and related material. You do not need to read the book in order.

Use this guide to help you identify, classify and resist the panopticons and pseudo-panopticons you come across in your daily life. An understanding of the genus is critical to understanding the ecology of surveillance culture.

We wish you luck,
Emily & Tim

'Morals reformed – health preserved – industry invigorated – instruction diffused – public burthens lightened – Economy seated, as it were, upon a rock – the Gordian knot of the Poor-Laws are not cut, but untied – all by a simple idea in Architecture!'

— Jeremy Bentham, *Panopticon; or,*
The Inspection-House

'Bentham was surprised that panoptic institutions could be so light: there were no more bars, no more chains, no more heavy locks; all that was needed was that the separations should be clear and the openings well arranged.'

— Michel Foucault, *Discipline & Punish*

Millbank Prison

The 1850 *Hand-Book of London*, a traveller's guidebook, describes Millbank Prison like this: 'A mass of brickwork equal to a fortress, on the left bank of the Thames, close to Vauxhall Bridge... It was designed by Jeremy Bentham, to whom the fee-simple of the ground was conveyed, and is said to have cost the enormous sum of half a million sterling.'

Millbank was still under construction when it opened in 1816. It was built on the marshy banks of the south side of the Thames, close enough to London for convenience but isolated enough to avoid complaints from neighbours. The layout was complex: a central tower was surrounded by a hexagon of walls, each segment of which was the base of a further pentagon of walls, with open exercise yards inside them. Each yard was watched over by its own four-storey tower. Seen from above in maps of the day, the prison resembles a barbed flower with six pentagonal petals, surrounded by a wall and moat that enclose the full sixteen-acre site.

It was a troubled project. The soggy terrain caused severe delays and cost two lead architects their jobs between 1812 and 1815. Budget overruns nearly doubled the original estimate of £259,700. Work was finally finished in 1821, but the prison didn't last long. Harsh conditions and surrounding marshland caused disease to sweep through the population, and an epidemic led to a complete evacuation in 1823. Even when people weren't getting sick, the design itself was fatally flawed. The labyrinthine network of corridors was so confusing that the prison's own warders sometimes got lost, and the echoing ventilation system transmitted sound so well that prisoners used it for illicit communication. By 1842, a newer prison, Pentonville, had been built to serve as the national penitentiary, and Millbank became a holding cell for convicts being shipped to Australia. It closed in 1890.

Bentham

The 1850 *Hand-Book of London* is wrong. Bentham did not design Millbank. As built, Millbank was designed by William Williams, drawing master at the Royal Military College, Sandhurst. It was the winning entry in a contest held to replace Bentham's design, the final insult after two decades of failed effort on Bentham's part to get his own revolutionary ideas set in stone.

It is true that Bentham tried to build a prison on the site. In 1794 he was paid £2,000 by British prime minister William Pitt for preliminary work on the project. Selection of the intended site ran into technical and legal problems that seemed to be resolved when Bentham, using government money, bought the land at Millbank in 1799. But the project faltered again, Pitt resigned from office in 1801 and in 1803 the new administration decided not to proceed. Hope was briefly restored in 1811, when the government returned to the idea, but Bentham became convinced there was no real commitment to the proposal. While Millbank was being built, Bentham was suing the government for wasting his best years. He settled for £23,000.

In Bentham's proposal, there was no labyrinth of corridors to get lost in, and no echoing ventilation system to allow for covert communication. His design – which he called the Panopticon – was an altogether purer affair. The complete idea was described over the course of twenty-one letters written from White Russia in 1787 to his father, an attorney back in England. They were collected and published as a single volume in 1791.

Bentham imagined a circular building, with the inspector's tower (or 'lodge,' as he preferred to call it) in the centre and the cells arranged radially around it. The central tower houses the prison warden and his family. Each four-sided cell is completely cut off from its neighbours. The interior side facing the lodge is open (aside from floor-to-ceiling bars) and the exterior side has a view to the outside world through a window on the outer wall. These windows are large enough that they light not only the cells, but the inspector's lodge as well. The play of darkness and light is important here: the windows of the lodge are protected by a fine metal grate that will allow the inspector to see into the lit cell, but prevents the prisoner from seeing into the relatively low-lit inspector's area. Blinds and partitions

Twenty-One Letters

further obscure the presence of the watcher. At night, artificial lights outside each window replicate the light of day so as to preserve this proto–one-way-mirror arrangement.

Panopticon; or The Inspection-House is a weird mixture of grand schemes and fine details. One moment, Bentham is talking about the distribution of profits from prison labour, and the next he's spending a half-dozen paragraphs working out how to run a system of gears through bent speaking tubes in order to drive a flag that will signal to prisoners that they're being talked to. Sometimes he's a salesman, sometimes a philosopher and sometimes a crank. He opens the letters with a bunch of hand-waving about the kind of stone and arches that would ensure the building will stay standing, and ends with a fanciful flight into imagining how the isolation systems of the Panopticon will allow you to raise and educate perfect virgin daughters to be ready for marriage. Not only the workings of light, but those of sound, heat and ventilation, are described in exacting detail.

Born in 1748, Jeremy Bentham was an English philosopher, social reformer and sometime lawyer, best known for his promulgation of the philosophy of utilitarianism. Utilitarianism preaches a moral framework based on encouraging actions that produce pleasure and discouraging those that produce pain. Acts that produce net pleasure must be good, and acts that produce net pain must be bad and ought to be avoided. Classical utilitarians like Bentham and John Stuart Mill (born 1806) were obsessed with the quantification of both joy and suffering, with the aim of producing institutions and social structures that minimized the latter.

Bentham – particularly in his later life – was a radical, advocating for women's equality, animal rights, separation of church and state, and the decriminalization of homosexuality. He was a fan of transparency and wanted people to be responsible for their own actions. He puts it like this in 1834's *Deontology*: 'It were to be wished that every man's name were written upon his forehead as well as engraved upon his door. It were to be wished that no such thing as secrecy existed – that every man's house were made of glass.' With transparency came accountability. 'The more men live in public,' he writes, 'the more amenable they are to the moral sanction.' The Panopticon was designed to make one particular class of people – convicted criminals – live very publicly.

Bentham's Panopticon is not just an exercise in radical transparency, it's also a labour-saving device. He's quite explicit on this point:

> I flatter myself there can now be little doubt of the plan's possessing the fundamental advantages I have been attributing to it: I mean, the *apparent omnipresence* of the inspector (if divines will allow me the expression,) combined with the extreme facility of his *real presence*.
>
> A collateral advantage it possesses, and on the score of frugality a very material one, is that which respects the *number* of the inspectors requisite. If this plan required more than another, the additional number would form an objection, which, were the difference to a certain degree considerable, might rise so high as to be conclusive: so far from it, that a greater multitude than ever were yet lodged in one house might be inspected by a single person; for the trouble of inspection is diminished in no less proportion than the strictness of inspection is increased.

From a central position of power, the unseen watchers potentially see all. The inmates, subjected to the whims of their guards and at peril of brutal reprisal for any wrongdoing, must assume they are being watched at all times. Because they are kept isolated, they are unable to coordinate any kind of resistance. They become their own jailers, forced into docility by clever construction techniques.

With such conditions persuading the prison's charges to self-discipline, fewer paid guards would be needed. It was also, Bentham believed, a less cruel solution than the alternative. In a classic win-win pitch, he argues that the Panopticon would reduce the costs of running the place (perfect security would allow you to get by with the thinnest of walls) while ending the need for restraining mechanisms like chains and irons.

> If you were to be asked who had most cause to wish for its adoption, you might find yourself at some loss to determine between the malefactors themselves, and those for whose sake they are consigned to punishment.
>
> In this view I am sure you cannot overlook the effect which it would have in rendering unnecessary that inexhaustible fund of disproportionate, too often needless, and always unpopular severity, not to say torture – the use of *irons*. Confined in one of these cells, every motion of the limbs, and every muscle of the face exposed to view, what pretence could there be for exposing to this hardship the most boisterous malefactor?

It must have galled Bentham to watch Millbank be built and fail as he pressed his suit against the government. That prison turned out to be essentially the anti-Panopticon. The thick walls and confusing layout weakened the warders' ability to monitor their charges, a problem only exacerbated by the badly designed ventilation system, allowing the convicts to coordinate and take liberties. Those liberties would have been met with the excesses of force from the guards and other unnecessary cruelties, leading to the harsh conditions that in turn led to the outbreak that caused the prison's evacuation.

No disease would have been allowed to proliferate in Bentham's Panopticon, like it did at Millbank. Bentham was certain that the Panopticon would have made an excellent hospital. In fact, Bentham saw the Panopticon as a one-size-fits-all solution for any institution. He had big dreams for his pet project, imagining it used for asylums, hospitals, factories, schools and workhouses:

> No matter how different, or even opposite the purpose: whether it be that of *punishing the incorrigible, guarding the insane, reforming the vicious, confining the suspected, employing the idle, maintaining the helpless, curing the sick, instructing the willing* in any branch of industry, or *training the rising race* in the path of *education*: in a word, whether it be applied to the purposes of *perpetual prisons* in the room of death, or *prisons for confinement* before trial, or *penitentiary-houses, or houses of correction, or work-houses, or manufactories, or mad-houses, or hospitals, or schools.*

The Panopticon was conceived as a universal instrument, endlessly flexible and able to mould its inhabitants in any way the administrators required.

Foucault

Michel Foucault elevated the panopticon from failed scheme to governing metaphor. Foucault was a French thinker, particularly interested in the structures and dynamics of power and knowledge. In 1975, he published *Surveiller et punir: Naissance de la prison*, known to us as *Discipline & Punish: The Birth of the Prison*.

Examining Bentham's plans, he saw those same labour-saving power structures woven into the fabric of 1970s society. In turn, academia followed Foucault, and the term *panopticon* was picked up and adopted in surveillance studies (a field of study that didn't truly begin until after Foucault's death, with Canadian sociologist David Lyon's work in the late 1980s), and eventually bled into common discourse. It is now more closely associated with Foucault than with Bentham, the idea's

A Word on Book Titles

Surveiller et punir: Naissance de la prison is better known to English speakers as *Discipline & Punish: The Birth of the Prison*. It's a funny kind of translation, given that we have *surveillance* in English. But for the 1977 English edition, translator Alan Sheridan decided that *surveiller* as used by the French had no exact Anglo equivalent. Sheridan rejected the most literal translation – *to* surveil – since *surveillance* was too technical and restricted a term. He also turned down *supervise* and *observe* for not having sharp enough teeth.

The French title is itself the child of translation. Foucault had translated Bentham's *inspect* as *surveiller*, but the new connotations Foucault gave to the Panopticon project don't really jive with *inspect* anymore. *Discipline* was Foucault's own suggestion, and Sheridan went along with it.

With the contemporary prevalence and ubiquity of *surveillance*, we suspect Sheridan might have made a different choice if he'd been translating in 2014 instead of 1977.

originator. Foucault brought the metaphor to bear on his own society and opened the door for generations of surveillance scholars to do the same.

For Foucault, the panopticon is the pinnacle of what he called the disciplinary society, the ideal that the Enlightenment rationalists of the eighteenth century were attempting to achieve. At the time, the outmoded practices of yesteryear were being rethought and replaced with new, rational solutions. The panopticon is the symbol for the shift from public punishment of criminals to the confinement and training of inmates, moulding them into good citizens. It has remained one of the most recognizable touchstones of Foucault's work, and consequently the most familiar part of Bentham's own philosophical output (with the possible exception of his willed request to have his skeleton mounted, clothed and displayed at University College London, which is pleasingly wacky).

In *Discipline & Punish*, Foucault traces the gradual changeover of penal practices in the eighteenth century. He contrasts the *ancien régime*'s public punishment with the disciplinary regime of confinement in prisons. (For historians, the *ancien régime* refers to the political and social system in France before the Revolution of 1789. Confusingly, Foucault borrows the name and reapplies it to mean European society in general during roughly that same period – this is just one of the reasons Foucault makes historians cranky.) In the *ancien régime*, punishment, torture and even death were meted out upon the criminal body, often before the observing masses. Foucault connects this type of practice to the former sovereign regimes of France, as the punishments were carried out under royal authority. The public execution is the ultimate expression of this system of administration. Punitive practice was performed in public to discourage further crime, and punishments were devised specifically to suit each crime. In the eighteenth century, Foucault says, there was a transition to a disciplinary society, where punishment was regularized and universalized No matter what the crime, the punishment is always confinement in a prison for a fixed duration of time. Now, rather than the body being punished directly, the body is imprisoned and it is the 'soul' of the prisoner that is submitted for improvement.

The panopticon is the inflexion point and the culmination point of this new regime. It is the platonic ideal of the control the disciplinary society is trying to achieve. Operation of the panopticon does not require special training or expertise; anyone (including the children or servants of the director, as Bentham suggests) can provide the observation that will produce the necessary effects of anxiety and paranoia in the prisoner. The building itself allows power to be instrumentalized, redirecting it to the accomplishment of specific goals, and the institutional architecture provides the means to achieve that end.

The operation of carceral power is not simple to apply, however. 'For this operation,' Foucault writes, 'the carceral apparatus has recourse to three great schemata: the politico-moral schema of individual isolation and hierarchy; the economic model of force applied to compulsory work; the technico-medical model of cure and normalization. The cell, the workshop, the hospital. The margin by which the prison exceeds detention is filled in fact by techniques of a disciplinary type. And this disciplinary addition to the juridical is what, in short, is called the "penitentiary."'

For instance, a boarding school relies on isolation and hierarchy, as well as compulsory work (the cell and the work-shop). An asylum works on the technico-medical level, as well as hierarchy, so it combines the hospital and the cell. A prison factory covers all three of the categories: inmates are confined and isolated from the general population, they are required to work, and their behaviours and health are moni-tored and normalized.

Power

Anyone reading Foucault will at least come out with this digestible nugget of his thought: power is a diffuse force, enacted and embodied by its users, existing in discourse. In Foucault's conception, power isn't concentrated in moments of coercion or domination, it is exerted constantly by everyone. Power is not applied only by leaders to ensure cooperation by underlings, it is practised by all.

His concept is so radical, it takes some effort to apply it to the panoptic prison. At first glance, it seems like the director in the panopticon clearly must have all the power: he is the one who looks. The prisoners are merely watched; they cannot even communicate amongst themselves. This looks like a classic, top-down coercive power structure. But Foucault thinks it describes the break from punitive 'sovereign' power and the shift to 'disciplinary' power. The objective of disciplinary power is to produce a docile, regulated and predictable body. Once someone is properly disciplined (by a combination of the physical architecture of the building and the surveillance it encourages, in the panopticon's case), she acts as her own jailer; she monitors herself.

Foucault was definitely opposed to the idea that power was concentrated in the specific people at the top of the pyramid. In *Discipline & Punish*, the power of the panopticon is distributed, and much of it resides in the building itself: 'Power has its principle not so much in a person as in a certain concerted distribution of bodies, surfaces, lights, gazes; in an arrangement whose internal mechanisms produce the relation in which individuals are caught up.'

So for Foucault, power is invested in the structure of the panopticon, rather than in the individuals who operate it. It makes the operation of power automatic, which in turn means that it's efficient to operate. It is the 'machinery' of the building that ensures the dissymmetry of visibility (and, thus, knowledge) that is required for its operation as a disciplinary institution.

Architecture

Foucault comes across as a pretty architectural thinker – *Discipline & Punish* is full of references to architectural forms: camps, mines, schools, hospitals, churches, prisons, squares, scaffolds. He's describing a world where the physical layout of buildings and institutions are used to modify behaviour. Architecture is crystallized power, and Foucault traces the emergence of this new purpose for architecture to the eighteenth century:

A whole problematic then develops: that of an architecture that is no longer built simply to be seen (as with the ostentation of palaces), or to observe external space (c.f. the geometry of fortresses), but to permit an internal, articulated and detailed control – to render visible those who are inside it; in more general terms, an architecture that would operate to transform individuals: to act on those it shelters, to provide a hold on their conduct, to carry the effects of power right to them, to make it possible to know them, to alter them. Stones can make people docile and knowable.

An interest in the tumultuous period around the seventeenth and eighteenth centuries in France informed Foucault's work until the end of his life, and ideas of space and architecture kept re-emerging. In a 1982 interview, Foucault said he found that discussions of architecture began to appear in political and governmental treatises (and even police reports!) in the eighteenth century. The shape of buildings and cities could help avoid epidemics and revolts, and even encourage morality. It was the opinion of those post-Napoleon reformers that architecture could solve the wider problems of the city, as well as the problems of the prison.

However, Foucault is clear that spatial reorganizations – even grand architectural plans – are not enough, that a building alone won't solve social problems. The plans of the architect must correspond with the practices of the people who inhabit that architecture, or the desired effect won't be achieved. 'I think that it can never be inherent in the structure of things to guarantee the exercise of freedom,' he writes. 'The guarantee of freedom is freedom.'

Surveillance

The guarantee of discipline is surveillance. For both Foucault and Bentham, the layout of space is a starting point, a technology that enhances a practice. Surveillance allows those in authority to know what is going on and to take steps to ensure ever finer degrees of control. The disciplinary society is typified by records, ledgers, performance reviews and logbooks. These make the bodies under the authority's care knowable.

'What is also of importance is, that for the greatest proportion of time possible, each man should actually *be* under inspection,' writes Bentham. 'This is material in *all* cases, that the inspector may have the satisfaction of knowing, that the discipline actually has the effect which it is designed to have: and it is more particularly material in such cases where the inspector, besides seeing that they conform to such standing rules as are prescribed, has more or less frequent occasion to give them such transient and incidental directions as will require to be given and enforced, at the commencement at least of every course of industry.'

In a disciplinary society, uniformity of outcome (be that education, military training, factory assembly or healing) requires a high personalization of intervention. 'It is not a triumphant power, which because of its own excess can pride itself on its omnipotence,' writes Foucault, 'it is a modest, suspicious power, which functions as a calculated, but permanent economy. These are humble modalities, minor procedures, as compared with the majestic rituals of sovereignty or the great apparatuses of the state.'

When a disciplinary society is operating at full potential, its members take on much of the work themselves. For Bentham, that meant prisoners coming to behave as if they were under constant observation, whether they were or not. For Foucault, that meant hierarchies of examiners, supervisors, monitors, tutors, foremen, clerks and similar functionaries efficiently gathering and transmitting information up and down the pyramids of power. Practice and surveillance become indistinguishable and individuals internalize the demands of the system in which they live.

Surveillance Studies

Surveillance studies is an interdisciplinary academic practice that tends to focus in the social sciences. Foucault is generally regarded as its source thinker. Of his many books, *Discipline & Punish* is the one most closely associated with surveillance culture, and the panopticon has been seized upon as a founding metaphor. Some expansions of the idea include: the 'Banopticon' (invented by professor Didier Bigo to describe profiling used to determine who deserves surveillance), 'electronic panopticon' (commonly used to describe today's surveillance technologies), 'myopic panopticon' (describing how CCTV detects only certain types of crime and may prevent even fewer), 'synopticon' (the surveillance of few by many) and, inevitably, the 'post-panopticon.'

Any time there is a leading thinker in a field, there is an intellectual backlash. Foucault's work has provoked ire from intellectuals across the spectrum, notably from Noam Chomsky, who holds a rationalist view of human nature as opposed to Foucault's anti-essentialist one; Jürgen Habermas, who had a problem with Foucault's amorphous conception of power; and Gertrude Himmelfarb, who in 1994 contested Foucault's reputation as a historian. (Foucault, for his part, had plenty of problems with historians, preferring to call his approach a genealogy.) Speaking specifically to surveillance, some academics are concerned about whether the panopticon metaphor still works for societies awash in surveillance from all directions rather than proceeding from a single, state-identified observer. Some surveillance scholars would rather see Foucault *and* his metaphor dead and buried.

However, as surveillance technologies proliferated throughout the twentieth century and into the twenty-first, not only surveillance scholars but journalists and popular writers seized upon the panopticon as a metaphor. To the everyday reader, it matters little that many in the academic world of surveillance studies have moved on from Foucault.

The architecture serves to enhance these relationships, but it's the surveillance that makes it all work. Given the tools of the day, a tower inside a ring that allowed easy line-of-sight observation was Bentham's best bet. Contemporary surveillance technologies permit a broader range of building layouts.

Schemes

No architectural project makes it to reality in its pure form. For speculative architects with utopian ideals, this can be a boon. Keeping such plans at the abstract, dreamlike level means never troubling yourself about whether something actually works. For Bentham, the Panopticon was intended to actually work, and he constantly refined its workings, relentlessly attentive to detail. That he was never permitted to actually build and run one was a bitter failure.

The fact that Bentham came close to building a panopticon is as important as the fact that he didn't. The various near-panopticons built around the world are a testament to the allure of his idea. Bentham himself would have predicted the failure of these buildings, including Millbank, as they ignored the details he had so painstakingly worked out. But in all likelihood, a panoptic institution built to Bentham's specifications wouldn't have worked as advertised, either.

'The Panopticon,' writes Foucault, 'must not be understood as a dream building: it is the diagram of a mechanism of power reduced to its ideal form; its functioning, abstracted from any obstacle, resistance or friction, must be represented as a pure architectural and optical system: it is in fact a figure of political technology that may and must be detached from any specific use.'

Now

Most of the evidence of Millbank Prison's seventy years of operation have been effaced. The site is currently occupied by the Tate Britain art gallery, which opened in 1897 (as the National Gallery of British Art), some seven years after the final closure of the prison. Some ghosts do remain: the underground isolation cells – called 'the Dark' – were uncovered during a gallery renovation, and the original outer perimeter walls and moat are discernible in the backyards of nearby turn-of-the-twentieth-century neighbourhoods.

More disturbing are the echoes of the panopticon in the daily life of the twenty-first century. Since Foucault's embrace of the panopticon as metaphor for surveillance and control, the mechanisms and prevalence of surveillance have run rampant. Everybody knows about the cameras, the National Security Agency monitoring and the drones. But the panopticon is about more than watching. We'd like to take you to a number of other instructive sites of contemporary control and power, and consider the relevance of Bentham's design and Foucault's ideas to their present operation.

This is a book about what Bentham was selling, what Foucault bought – and says we all bought – and why Foucault seems especially relevant today.

Pseudo-Panopticons

We have made the claim that no panopticon has ever been built. We do not make this claim lightly, having spent some time searching for a 'real' panopticon before settling on Millbank. Just like Millbank, there are many prisons (and a few other types of institutions) said to have been built on panoptic principles. Mostly, what this seems to mean is that they're circular. But a circular plan does not a panopticon make. A true panoptic institution should allow full, anonymous viewing of the inmates, be open to the public for inspection, minimize contact between prisoners and reduce the number of guards required to run the place. To achieve full marks, it should also be run according to the principles set down by Bentham (he spends as much time working out those policies as he does on the actual layout, after all). Here are the candidates we rejected:

Edinburgh Bridewell (1795): Scotland's first penitentiary, it was designed by Robert Adam. His original plan was a standard neoclassical building, but after a meeting with Bentham, he changed his mind. The sleeping quarters for prisoners were not visible from the centre of the semicircular structure, but their working areas were.

St. Petersburg Panopticon Institute, Russia (1809): Jeremy's own brother, Samuel Bentham, had a naval trade school built for youths aged seven to twenty-two on a panoptic plan. The workhouse burned down in 1818.

Round House, Australia (1831): The Round House prison was opened only eighteen months after the settlement of the state of Western Australia. A well and an open courtyard are surrounded by eight cells and guards' quarters. While it was designed by the son of an architect collaborator of Bentham's, this small jail makes a weak case for being panoptic, as the guards' rooms were not central and it had so few cells.

Mobile Panopticon (1837): Foucault describes the July Monarchy's replacement for the chain gang as 'a carriage conceived as a moving prison, a mobile equivalent of the Panopticon.' Prisoners were transported in the back of the wagon in individual cells, with grilles for surveillance. While Foucault indicates that prisoners were chastened by their sleepless travels in the carriage, it couldn't have been that great since it wasn't in use for very long.

Three domed panoptic prisons in the Netherlands, at Breda and Arnhem (1886) and Haarlem (1901), the first two designed by J. F. Metzelaar and the last by his son, W. C. Metzelaar. These circular buildings with stacked cells (four hundred of them, in the case of Haarlem) were in operation for over one hundred years, and will all be closed by 2016. They fail as true panopticons since the guards could not see the entire cell at all times, due to the small size of the window in each cell door.

Pavilhão de Segurança, Portugal (1896): An asylum for mentally ill prisoners, it is now a museum, integrated into the Psychiatric Hospital of Lisbon. The central courtyard was meant to allow for the inmates to spend time outside in healthful fresh air. While it's undeniably striking as a building, it still lacks full visibility of the patients in their rooms.

Bogota Panóptico, Colombia (1874): Designed by Thomas Reed, it now houses the National Museum. The form of the building is a cross encircled by an outer circular wall, so it has more in common with the radial prison designs of the nineteenth century, which allowed guards to see down hallways, but not into individual cells.

Isla de la Juventud, Cuba (1928): This huge prison was built by dictator Gerardo Machado and housed up to 2,500 prisoners at a time in five circular cellblocks, each with a tall central observation tower. After the Cuban Revolution, the prison housed up to eight thousand political prisoners, and was the site of riots and hunger strikes. Visually, this prison is a strong panopticon contender, but Bentham would never have stood for the overcrowding.

Chí Hòa Prison, Vietnam (1943): This three-floor octagonal building was begun by the French colonial government but has been used by all succeeding regimes. A central guard tower overlooks the cells and exercise yard. Prisoners were often fettered, which runs counter to the idea of the Panopticon, in which good behaviour is ensured by vigilance rather than irons.

Lelystad Prison, Netherlands (2006): Designed by J. C. Putter, this prison uses locative technology for today's digital panopticon. Prisoners are tagged, and these tags send a signal every two seconds, tracking the prisoner's location. This design means that only six guards are needed for 150 prisoners, rather than the standard fifteen or more. Jeremy Bentham is loving this one (except these prisoners sleep six to a room!).

'I will not pester you with further niceties applicable to the difference between *houses of correction*, and *work-houses*, and *poor-houses*, if any there should be, which are not work-houses; between the different modes of treatment that may be due to what are looked upon as the inferior degrees of *dishonesty*, to *idleness* as yet untainted with dishonesty, and to blameless *indigence*. The law herself has scarcely eyes for these microscopic differences. I bow down, therefore, for the present at least, to the counsel of so many sages, and shrink from the crime of being "wiser than the law."'

— Jeremy Bentham, *Panopticon; or, The Inspection-House*

'The labour by which the convict contributes to his own needs turns the thief into a docile worker. This is the utility of remuneration for penal labour; it imposes on the convict the "moral" form of wages as the condition of his existence.'

— Michel Foucault, *Discipline & Punish*

We want to tell you about Tim's new jeans. They cost twenty-eight dollars. They're called Prison Blues. They are a kind of charismatic megafauna from a strange and complex ecosystem. They might be a heraldic emblem for an old and unresolved debate about what should happen to people who go to prison.

Every brand has a story. With jeans, that story is often stapled to the back pocket on a piece of cardboard that you throw away before you put them on. Here's the full text on the back pocket of Tim's jeans:

YES. THEY'RE REALLY MADE IN PRISON.

Prison Blues®. The original, authentic, prison-constructed blue jean brand. Manufactured by inmates at the Eastern Oregon Correctional Institution in Pendleton, Oregon, U.S.A.

By men who aren't necessarily your stereotypical hardened criminals — they're fathers, sons, and brothers interested in making amends for the choices that put them behind bars. And they make some of the most durable denim clothes that you'll ever lay your hands on.

Find them. Check out that durable Fabric. Peruse that careful stitching. Feel that fit.

Weld in them. Fall timber. Build houses. Haul. Dig in the dirt. You have the freedom to choose.

Made to do hard time.
Visit us at www.prisonblues.com for the story.

When Tim's jeans arrived, that URL didn't actually work. Indeed, as we tried to find out more of the Prison Blues story, we encountered a trail of seemingly abandoned websites and dead links. We don't think this is because they're trying to hide what they do or anything, we just think they're bad at internet.

Tim bought the jeans at allamericanstore.us. Its URL works just fine.

On the front page, in big bold type, it says, 'Welcome to America's largest retail company selling products Made in the USA and proudly Handcrafted in America.' It offers free shipping to everywhere in the continental United States. The top of the website features a heroic angle shot of the Statue of Liberty in front of a blurry, fluttering American flag. The slogan is 'Building America One Purchase At A Time.'

To what extent the jeans may be helpful or harmful to American industry, the website does not say, though it does assure us on the product page that '*80% of wages earned by inmates is contributed into a victim's relief fund.*'

The jeans were made at the Eastern Oregon Correctional Institution in Pendleton, Oregon. The site is a former insane asylum built in 1912 and converted into a prison in 1985. It looks nothing like a panopticon. The main building consists of two symmetrical sets of staggered wings reminiscent of Thomas Story Kirkbride's iconic designs. Several smaller buildings and some later additions are scattered around the site, including two baseball fields. Pendleton's population is about 16,000. The prison has 1,600 beds. According to the prison's official web page, it is the town's fourth-largest employer.

The Prison Blues brand is owned by Oregon Corrections Enterprises, a semi-independent body – the administrator reports directly to the Oregon Department of Corrections – which was established in 1999. OCE employs 1,200 inmates at any given time, and these days Oregon is housing about 14,000 inmates. Most prison labour goes toward jobs within the prison – laundry services, groundskeeping, kitchen work and the like.

Financially, OCE is having some trouble. Although it is intended to be self-sustaining, revenue has been uneven; successful laundry and call-centre services meant the program posted a $1.8 million profit in 2012, but it lost $700,000 the following year. In a 2013 report, the Portland State University's Center for Public Service (CPS) warned that 'OCE's current major revenue streams – furniture manufacturing, laundry services, and call centres – face significant and increasing competition from private and non-profit entities.'

Part of the problem for OCE's finances is that it is trapped in an impossible situation. In 1994, Oregon voters passed the Prison Reform and Inmate Work Act, a constitutional amendment requiring that all inmates should work forty hours per week. Everyone in prison (a population that has doubled since 1994) is expected to work. But the law that governs OCE says it must 'avoid establishing or expanding for-profit prison work programs that produce goods or services offered for sale in the private sector if the establishment or expansion would displace or significantly reduce preexisting private enterprise' or 'displace or significantly reduce government or nonprofit programs that employ persons with developmental disabilities.'

So, everyone has to work, and an independent, semi-private agency that is meant to be self-funding has been set up to employ some of them, but it had better not compete with any companies on the outside! This impossible demand is typical of the outcome of debates around prison labour. Those debates stretch back to the birth of prisons.

The jeans are not represented in the CPS report's list of major revenue streams. In many ways, Prison Blues are strange exceptions. It is hard for consumers to acquire prison-made goods in America. For the most part, prisons sell to institutional clients. UNICOR – the federal equivalent of OCE – makes clothing and armour for the U.S. military, dormitory beds and mattresses, industrial signage and lockers, and a range of office furniture. When you visit the website for its textile division, you are confronted with an immediate warning: 'By law, UNICOR may only sell its products to Federal departments, agencies, government institutions, and their authorized contractors or representatives.' And so, for the most part, if consumers are going to interact directly with prison labour, it's going to be unwittingly, through a call centre that employs convicts.

To immerse yourself in the conflict about prison labour is to feel completely unstuck in time. The arguments for and against prison labour and the rhetoric around the dispute have remained more or less unchanged over the last three hundred years. For instance, regardless of when their opinions were written, people in favour of labour in prisons are overwhelmingly worried about idleness. Foucault spends a fair bit of time in *Discipline & Punish* talking about this, pulling lines from documents written in the 1800s and comparing them to (then-contemporary) debates around prison reform in the 1970s. In 1945, a commission headed by Paul Amor, first director of l'Administration pénitentiaire française, studied the appalling conditions of French prisons and proposed fourteen principles to improve them. Those included a section on work, which sets up prison labour as both a right (no prisoner can be forced to be idle) and an obligation (all prisoners are required to work). Foucault mentions the prisoner revolts that were happening while he was writing in the early 1970s, and suggests they occurred because the 'reforms proposed in 1945 never really took effect.'

Here's what the 1808 French Code of Criminal Instruction has to say about work in prison:

> Although the penalty inflicted by the law has as its aim the reparation of a crime, it is also intended to reform the convict, and this double aim will be fulfilled if the

malefactor is snatched from that fatal idleness which, having brought him to prison, meets him again...

Here's how Judge J. Brandeis discussed prison labour in 1922:

Work must be one of the essential elements in the transformation and progressive socialization of convicts. Penal labour 'must not be regarded as the complement and as it were an aggravation of the penalty, but as a mitigation, of which it is no longer possible to deprive the prisoner.'

Here's how Morgan O. Reynolds of the Dallas-based National Center for Policy Analysis wrote about it in 1996:

Despite a consensus of the American public that prison inmates should be gainfully employed, most are idle. Their idleness contrasts sharply with the circumstances of their 19th-century counterparts. Three-fourths worked and two-thirds of the workers were contracted to private entrepreneurs and farmers to produce goods for the general marketplace.

And here is how the government of Oregon's website explains OCE's programs today:

Many inmates come to prison having never held a real job or learned the value of work. Oregon Corrections Enterprises (OCE) was designed to serve Oregon citizens by providing inmates hands-on vocational training and teaching pro-social values including work ethics, responsibility, and a sense of self-worth they lost or never before experienced. Through work experience, OCE facilitates inmates' adjustment and reintegration into Oregon communities upon their release. With this in mind, inmate work assignments emulate real-life to the greatest extent possible.

If you want to speak for the pro–prison-labour side, here are your talking points:

- Labour gives prisoners something to do, which they prefer to idleness.
- It teaches them the value of an honest day's work.
- It gives them training and skills for their life on the outside, reducing recidivism.
- It controls behaviour and reduces discipline issues on the inside.
- It helps offset the costs of incarcerating people.
- Prisoners are a resource that should not be left unexploited.
- Prisoners should not get a free ride in jail.

One of the great pendulums of history swings between whether prison should be a place for rehabilitation or a place for retribution. Weirdly, no matter where on that scale a thinker finds herself, she can be in favour of prison labour. For the rehabilitators, prison labour helps people learn skills and reduces boredom. For the retributionists, hard labour is a fitting punishment. How work can be both of these things at once is rarely addressed.

If you want to speak *against* prison labour, here are your talking points:

- It hurts free workers through unfairly depressing wages.
- It hurts private business through unfairly cheap goods.
- It takes resources away from law-abiding people.
- It is tantamount to slavery.

Opposition to prison labour often comes from working-class populations outside the prison who worry about their own wages being driven down. This opposition is strongest in times of economic hardship – for example, it spiked in the U.S. after the Civil War and during the Great Depression.

Rather than trying to unite with their fellow workers inside prison walls, the outside working-class agitators laboured against them. In the late nineteenth and early twentieth centuries, racial differences between a largely white, non-imprisoned working class and a largely black prison population exacerbated the rift.

Depressingly, the slavery argument is the one that seems to get used the least often. In America, the refusal to equate forced labour inside a prison's walls to forced labour outside of them is particularly pronounced. When the U.S. amended its Constitution for the thirteenth time in 1865 to ban slavery, it explicitly reaffirmed prison labour as totally okay: 'Neither slavery nor involuntary servitude, except as a punishment for crime whereof the party shall have been duly convicted, shall exist within the United States, or any place subject to their jurisdiction.'

This has repeatedly caused problems for prisoners seeking redress. When prisoners in Georgia used smuggled cellphones to coordinate a strike in 2010, their first demand was 'A LIVING WAGE FOR WORK: In violation of the 13th Amendment to the Constitution prohibiting slavery and involuntary servitude, the DOC demands prisoners work for free.' Not that it ever got to court, but if it had, legal tradition emanating from the Thirteenth Amendment means they would have had a hard time pressing their case. Here's a piece of that tradition: in the 1871 case of Ruffin v. Commonwealth, the Virginia Supreme Court went so far as to call prisoners 'slaves of the state':

'A convicted felon, whom the law in its humanity punishes by confinement in the penitentiary instead of with death, is subject while undergoing that punishment, to all the laws which the Legislature in its wisdom may enact for the government of that institution and the control of its inmates. For the time being, during

Ten Chapters in Four Sections

PART ONE   TORTURE
1. The body of the condemned
2. The spectacle of the scaffold

PART TWO   PUNISHMENT
1. Generalized punishment
2. The gentle way in punishment

PART THREE   DISCIPLINE
1. Docile bodies
     The art of distributions
     The control of activity
     The organization of geneses
     The composition of forces
2. The means of correct training
     Hierarchical observation
     Normalizing judgment
     The examination
3. Panopticism

PART FOUR   PRISON
1. Complete and austere institutions
2. Illegalities and delinquency
3. The carceral

his term of service in the penitentiary, he is in a state of penal servitude to the State. He has, as a consequence of his crime, not only forfeited his liberty, but all his personal rights except those which the law in its humanity accords to him. He is for the time being the slave of the State.'

The courts have since walked back from that position, though they have steadily held a wide interpretation of what counts as punishment in the context of the Thirteenth Amendment. One reading of the Thirteenth would be that people can be put to work only if their sentence specifically names involuntary servitude. In that narrow reading, the amendment allows hard labour as a punishment but not a general policy. The courts have instead chosen to read the amendment as allowing forced labour for anyone sent to jail.

In the U.S., the courts have a policy of deferring to prison officials on the day-to-day running of a prison (it's called the 'due-deference' or 'hands-off' doctrine). This was most explicitly articulated by Supreme Court Justice William Rehnquist in 1979 in a case about the leeway that prison officials had to conduct body-cavity searches, restrict reading material and double-bunk pretrial detainees: 'Finally, as the Court of Appeals correctly acknowledged, the problems that arise in the day-to-day operation of a corrections facility are not susceptible of easy solutions. Prison administrators therefore should be accorded wide-ranging deference in the adoption and execution of policies and practices that in their judgment are needed to preserve internal order and discipline and to maintain institutional security.'

The hands-off doctrine means that a lot of the privations of prison life come not as a result of the sentence handed down by a court, but as a result of policies and practices set up by the prisons. Far from the promise of constitutional protections, brutal living conditions, overcrowding, and health and safety issues end up being justified on the basis of budgetary problems or bad building design.

Foucault saw this coming. 'All this "arbitrariness" which, in the old penal system, enabled the judges to modulate the penalty and the princes to ignore it if they so wished,' he writes, 'all this arbitrariness, which the modern codes have withdrawn from the judicial power, has been gradually reconstituted on the side of the power that administers and supervises punishment.'

No court would sentence a person to sexual assault, starvation, beatings, inadequate medical care or death by stabbing, and yet these incidents are common enough to be part of the pop-cultural mythology about what happens in prison. It is accepted and understood that prisoners are accorded privileges and punishments according to the judgments of their jailer. Some people end up in solitary confinement, some end up doing yardwork and some end up making jeans – these are very different lives.

The Thirteenth Amendment is a direct consequence of America's Civil War, so let's talk about the Late Unpleasantness for a moment. More to the point, let's talk about cotton, which is what Tim's jeans are made of.

When the Confederate States of America seceded from the Union in 1861, it was specifically to maintain the institution of slavery. They feared that efforts to block slavery from spreading to the new states in the west would in turn lead to the abolition of slavery throughout the entire U.S. The South knew it could not win its war alone. Just as the 1776 War of Independence was won with support and recognition from France, the South believed it could fight the Union off long enough to secure support from France or Britain – support that would come because of the industrialized world's reliance on cotton.

King Cotton, they called it. It was a keystone material of the industrial revolution kicked off in the U.K. by textile manufacturing sometime between 1760 and 1780, depending on which historian you ask. Whatever the date, when Bentham was writing *Panopticon* in 1787, the revolution was well underway. The flying shuttle, invented in 1733 and reaching widespread use by 1760, had driven demand for spun cotton, which in turn led to the inventions of the spinning jenny, the water frame and, finally, the spinning mule in 1779.

The consequences of all this automation were strange. In England, you get the standard story of mechanization: the faster and more efficient machines drove down prices, and destroyed the livelihoods of human labourers. Fears that all the machines were destroying livelihoods led to the rise of groups like the Luddites. But in the U.S., things ran differently. It is difficult to find two sources that agree on the precise figures, but thankfully, orders of magnitude overwhelm all error. Here are the approximate rates of U.S. cotton production leading up to the Civil War:

1791: 4,000 bales of cotton
1820: 400,000 bales
1860: 4,000,000 bales – accounting for 57 percent of U.S. export revenue

The key year is 1793, when Eli Whitney invented the cotton gin. Before Whitney's reliable solution, getting the seeds and other not-good-for-fabric stuff out of cotton was a painstaking manual process. After the gin, which offered a fiftyfold increase in speed, processing was no longer the limiting factor. Instead, the limit was the amount of available land, which, in the southern U.S. was, like, all of it. While the gin had automated the first step of cotton processing, there was no mechanical solution to growing and picking cotton. That still needed human labour.

As Bentham was writing *Panopticon*, slavery in the U.S. seemed be on its way out and cotton was an economically unimportant crop. While Bentham was suing the British government over Millbank, cotton production had metastasized and demand for slaves had expanded to meet the needs of the highly scalable production lines. Better automation meant more slaves. The industrial revolution was supplied by slaves.

The Civil War ended in 1865. In 1873, tailor Jacob Davis and dry-goods wholesaler Levi Strauss were awarded U.S. Patent No. 139,121 – an 'Improvement in fastening pocket-openings' by using copper rivets to reinforce the seams on the cotton pants that had become known as jeans.

The end of the Civil War officially meant the end of involuntary servitude in the U.S. The sudden loss of an enslaved population was a significant shock to the economy, and the southern states moved quickly to cushion the blow. One strategy focused on exploiting that one exception to the Thirteenth Amendment – prison labour. Across the South, states passed a set of laws that together became known as the convict lease system. It was exactly what it sounds like. Here, let Morgan O. Reynolds, writing for the pro–privatized-prison-labour National Center for Policy Analysis, explain:

> After the Civil War, convict leases became another way in which prisoners were put to work. Under convict leases, private employers essentially assumed control over nearly all aspects of prison life, including security and living conditions. Prisoner leases usually involved work camps on farms, construction sites (including railroads) and mines outside prison walls. Leases to private employers usually yielded the highest revenues to the state.

Perhaps the wording of a memorandum that establishes one of the first convict leases will make this clearer. Thomas H. Ruger, military governor of Georgia, is writing to William Fort of the Georgia and Alabama Railroad. Ruger promises Fort 'one hundred able bodied and healthy Negro convicts now confined in the said Penitentiary' to work for a year. In return, Fort would cover all expenses for keeping the prisoners and pay the state $2,500.

Laws that made these arrangements possible, plus laws that made it easy to imprison freed blacks for crimes like vagrancy, resulted in a surge in the African-American prison population in the South. The overall population started to climb, and the proportion of black prisoners climbed faster. They were in turn leased out to work in factories, mines and plantations. In several cases, the revenue from leased people became a significant chunk of state income during Reconstruction. In the case of Alabama, it accounted for 73 percent of the state's budget in 1898.

'Leasing proved economically successful but politically difficult,' Reynolds laments. Yes. That is because the southern states had re-implemented slavery. In one notorious incident, (white) North Dakota resident Martin Tabert was arrested for vagrancy in Florida and ordered to pay twenty-five dollars or face three months' hard labour. His family sent fifty dollars (the extra cash was to cover his return home), but through 'mishandling' the money never made it. In 1921, Tabert was flogged to death at a labour camp run by the Putnam Lumber Company.

Reynolds has a lot to say in favour of privatized prison labour and draws inspiration from a familiar figure: 'In 1787 the founding father of criminology in the English-speaking world, Jeremy Bentham...urged replacement of the jails of his day by what he termed "mills for grinding rogues honest and idle men industrious."' And so we come back to Bentham's plan. The design of the Panopticon is intimately tied to the question of labour. Remember here that the Panopticon is intended as a gentler and more just alternative to other imprisonment schemes. The idea is that surveillance would replace shackles, but the physical construction of the Panopticon is part of a much larger and more comprehensive system.

Bentham devotes just under half of his letters about the Panopticon to the economic and labour policies that would make it work. His idea is that the institution would attract a private contractor to run it because it would be self-funding by putting convicts to work for free. How to get them to work for free? Simple. Provide them with the barest necessities and leave them isolated in their cells. '[T]here the man is in his dungeon already (the only sort of dungeon, at least, which I conceive any man need be in,) very safe and quiet,' writes Bentham. 'He is likewise entertaining himself with his bread and water, with only one little circumstance in his favour, that whenever he is tired of that regimen, it is in his own power to put himself under a better.' Or, as one of Reynolds's section titles puts it in 1996, 'Prisoners Overwhelmingly Prefer Work to the Tedium of Prison Life.'

Bentham goes on to suggest that once that relationship has been established, it might continue past the end of the convict's jail term. 'No trade that could be carried on in this state of thraldom, but could be carried on with at least equal advantage in a state of liberty,' he writes. 'Both parties would probably find their account in continuing their manufacturing connexion, after the dissolution of every other. The workman, after the stigma cast on him by the place of his abode, would probably not find it so easy to get employment elsewhere.'

Though OCE does not employ prisoners once they have left the custody of the state, as we saw earlier, it does conceive of itself as preparing them with valuable skills. Given the decline of America's textile industry (the U.S. is now the world's third-largest cotton producer and 65 percent of the crop is exported), it is not clear how much brighter a convict's prospects became after making Tim's jeans.

The link between the panopticon and manufacturing runs deep. In fact, the panopticon wasn't originally conceived as a prison design. It was conceived as a factory, and not by Jeremy Bentham, but by his brother, Samuel. Samuel Bentham went to Russia in 1780 to look for work as a naval engineer. For a while, he worked for an English manufactory in St. Petersburg, and then toured the Urals in 1781–1782. By 1784, Samuel

Bentham was working on Prince Grigory Potemkin's estate at Krichev. (Yes, *that* Potemkin.)

Potemkin was in the midst of industrializing the countryside, building villages and factories in anticipation of Catherine the Great's upcoming grand tour through the southern parts of her territory. Bentham had unlimited funds to improve the estate, but he had a labour problem – there weren't enough skilled workers in the area. He imported English craftsmen to teach the Russian serfs the necessary skills in boat-building and manufacturing. That led to discipline issues, not among the Russian workers, but their English supervisors. Bentham's deputy listed their shortcomings as follows: 'laziness, thievery, quarrelling, drinking.'

Samuel's design of what he called the Inspection House (or Elaboratory) wasn't so much concerned with watching the labourers as it was with supervising the supervisors. The design was built around Samuel Bentham's own residence in the centre, with the workforce arrayed around him, available at any time for his careful inspection.

In 1786, brother Jeremy joined Samuel on a writing retreat. He was so struck by Samuel's plans that he worked them up into a prison plan in response to a competition to design a new penitentiary for Middlesex. He sent those plans back to his father in England, where they were eventually published as *Panopticon; or, The Inspection-House* in 1791. It was Jeremy who retrofitted the factory design and then made the Panopticon universally applicable to any institution requiring discipline, and it is that adaptability that fascinates us (as well as Foucault).

Security Bulletin: Reportable Information
Published in *The Wire, the Official Publication of Joint Task Force Guantanamo, March 2, 2007*

The security of classified information is of the highest importance to our nation's defense. The safeguarding of our secrets ensures protection of missions, operations, and personnel. This process depends upon the continuous evaluation of employees who have been granted access to classified information. To remain qualified for a security clearance, all personnel are required to be continually assessed for standards of conduct, patterns of behavior, affiliations, and allegiance. Individuals who become aware of unfavorable information about another individual are required to report that information to the Command Security Manager or Special Security Office.

Unfavorable or potentially disqualifying information can come to the attention of anyone in the supervisory chain, working or social environment. Once the information surfaces, it is every recipient's responsibility to ensure that it is reported appropriately.

Unfavorable or disqualifying information falls into the following categories:

a. Allegiance to the United States.

b. Foreign influence.

c. Foreign preference.

d. Sexual behavior.

e. Personal conduct.

f. Financial considerations.

g. Alcohol consumption.

h. Drug involvement

i. Emotional, mental, and personality disorders.

j. Criminal conduct.

k. Security violations.

l. Outside activities.

m. Misuse of information technology systems.

Supervisors and commanders must ensure their personnel are aware of their responsibility to report unfavorable information, maintain high standards of trustworthiness and loyalty, and avoid any personal behavior that would result in rendering themselves ineligible for a security clearance.

Failure to report unfavorable or disqualifying information can be grounds for loss of security clearance for both the individual and of the person failing to report. The reporting of unfavorable information will not necessarily result in the individual's security clearance being suspended. The information provided will be considered in conjunction with other factors, to include the individual's previous record, recommendations of the supervisor, and mitigating circumstances.

Mission first, security always!

'Overpowering the guard requires an union of hands, and a concert among minds. But what union, or what concert, can there be among persons, no one of whom will have set eyes on any other from the first moment of his entrance?'

— Jeremy Bentham, *Panopticon; or,*
The Inspection-House

'The public execution was the logical culmination of a procedure governed by the Inquisition. The practice of placing individuals under "observation" is a natural extension of a justice imbued with disciplinary methods and examination procedures.'

— Michel Foucault, *Discipline & Punish*

Foucault opens *Discipline & Punish* with a before-and-after. First he describes — in excruciating detail — the 1757 execution by torture of Damiens the regicide. Then he quotes from Léon Faucher's 1837 rules for the 'House of young prisoners in Paris.' The rules are far more stately, listing in minute detail the schedule of the day and how prisoners are to behave. 'We have, then, a public execution and a time-table,' writes Foucault. 'They do not punish the same crimes or the same type of delinquent. But they each define a certain penal style. Less than a century separates them.'

'You have asked for our Office's views concerning the effect of international treaties and federal laws on the treatment of individuals detained by the U.S. Armed Forces during the conflict in Afghanistan,' writes Deputy Assistant Attorney General John Yoo in a 2002 memo to William J. Haynes II, General Counsel, U.S. Department of Defense. 'In particular, you have asked whether the laws of armed conflict apply to the conditions of detention and the procedures for trial of members of al Qaeda and the Taliban militia. We conclude that these treaties do not protect members of the al Qaeda organization, which as a non-State actor cannot be a party to the international agreements governing war. We further conclude that these treaties do not apply to the Taliban militia.'

In the popular press, Yoo's work becomes known as one of the Torture Memos.

In Foucault's recounting, the torture of Damiens the regicide is a botched execution. The sulphur does not light properly and so Damiens's hand is barely burned. The executioner's pincers — specially made for the occasion — don't do a good job of tearing off Damiens's skin. The horses are not up to the job of drawing and quartering, and after several failed attempts, the executioners have to get permission to cut his limbs to the bone so the horses have an easier time. But though the execution was botched, it was not chaotic brutality. A procedure was followed. There was a recipe for the mixture of molten lead, boiling oil, burning resin, wax and sulphur melted together and poured over Damiens's wounds. There was a specific order of events. There was a priest on hand to hear his confession.

In a 2005 memo to John A. Rizzo, Senior Deputy General Counsel, Central Intelligence Agency, Steven G. Bradbury, Principal Deputy Assistant Attorney General, Department of Justice, addresses 'whether certain specified interrogation techniques designed to be used on a high value al Qaeda detainee in the War on Terror comply with the federal prohibition on torture.' Bradbury notes that while torture is 'abhorrent both to American law and values,' his task is complicated 'by the lack of precision in the statutory terms and the lack of relevant case law.'

Bradbury also notes that any detainee who undergoes enhanced interrogation is evaluated by medical and psychological professionals who work for the CIA 'to ensure that he is not likely to suffer any severe physical or mental pain or suffering as a result of interrogation.' The techniques in turn are to be used in an escalating fashion, beginning with milder ones. Once approval is given, enhanced interrogation techniques can be used for thirty days without further approval needed, and medical and psychological personnel are on-scene throughout. 'This memorandum addresses the use of these techniques during no more than one 30-day period. We do not address whether the use of these techniques beyond the initial 30-day period would violate the statute,' Bradbury writes.

Here are the techniques considered: *dietary manipulation* (nutritionally adequate but bland food); *nudity* (without sexual innuendo on the part of interrogators); *attention grasp* (grabbing the prisoner by the collar); *walling* (slamming the prisoner against a false wall designed to make a loud noise – this may happen once per session or twenty to thirty times), *facial hold* (fingers are kept well away from the individual's eyes); *facial slap* (this 'invades the individual's "personal space"'); *abdominal slap* (a backhanded slap – 'the interrogator must have no rings or other jewelry'); *cramped confinement* ('duration of confinement varies based on the size of the container'); *wall standing; stress positions* (three positions – 'like wall standing, they are designed to produce the physical discomfort associated with temporary muscle fatigue'); *water dousing* (the water must be potable and the detainee can't stay wet for longer than two-thirds the time that medical literature says hypothermia would set in); *flicking water; sleep deprivation* (prisoners are kept awake from forty-eight to 180 hours, shackled standing up or sometimes on a small stool); *the waterboard* ('We understand the effect of the waterboard is to induce the sensation of drowning' – 'a physician and a psychologist are present at all times').

Bradbury ultimately concludes that these techniques do not constitute torture. He does, however, urge caution in the case of sleep deprivation and waterboarding, including both 'careful adherence to the limitations and safeguards imposed' and also 'constant monitoring by both medical and psychological personnel.'

Foucault calls the era that surrounds Damiens's execution the *ancien régime*. He takes the name used for the administrative, judicial and ecclesiastic structures of the pre-revolutionary Kingdom of France and repurposes it as shorthand for the broader social, political and juridical structures across European civilization at the time. He emphasizes that though the practices of judicial torture were cruel, they were not wild:

Judicial torture was not a way of obtaining the truth at all costs; it was not the unrestrained torture of modern interrogations; it was certainly cruel, but it was not savage. It was a regulated practice, obeying a well-defined procedure; the various stages, their duration, the instruments used, the length of ropes and the heaviness of the weights used, the number of interventions made by the interrogating magistrate, all this was, according to the different local practices, carefully codified...the 'patient' – this is the term used to designate the victim – was subjected to a series of trials, graduated in severity, in which he succeeded if he 'held out,' or failed if he confessed.

The era typified by Faucher's rules is better understood as a disciplinary society. It slackens its hold on the body, says Foucault, while tightening its grip on the mind. The workings of power are moved away from grand public spectacle and toward minute mechanisms of control woven into the social fabric and the very architecture we inhabit. Foucault takes Bentham's Panopticon as his organizing metaphor.

Barely a decade separates the Guantanamo Bay that led John Yoo to write his memos from the one that artist and journalist Molly Crabapple visited in 2013. The days of torture are over. 'Guantanamo Bay is where people wait,' Crabapple writes for *Medium*. 'A faded relic of The War on Terror, four of its eight camps stand empty for lack of prisoners.' Five years after President Obama first ordered the camp shut down, it is still open, housing 149 detainees, seventy-eight of whom have been approved for release. The U.S. base sits on 120 square kilometres of land and sea at the southeastern tip of the island of Cuba. The various military installations are placed around the bay itself, including two airfields, a courthouse, housing and schools for personnel, recreation facilities and, of course, the prison complex.

Tours of duty for GTMO's guards last nine to twelve months. With the exception of the camp's cultural advisor (pseudonym Zak, 'whose job,' writes Crabapple, 'is to teach guards about the Muslim Mind, and [vice] versa'), none of the current regime were present for the application of the techniques approved by Bradbury and Yoo.

Detainees are visually inspected via cell CCTV cameras every three minutes. Bentham's panoptic mechanism relies on an extreme asymmetry of visibility; the guards are rarely or never visible to the inmates, and the inmates are constantly available to be looked at by the guards. Foucault took that practical concept and made it about knowledge and power; power in the panopticon is 'visible and unverifiable.' The CCTV camera is always visible to the detainee, standing in for his guard's unverifiable inspecting eye.

In another article written for *Vice*, Crabapple describes the security procedures, which are painstakingly elaborate. As we learn about the measures imposed on visitors, detainees and guards, the insistence on the one-way transfer of information begins to take on a ritualistic feel. Visitors are scrupulously searched and all electronics removed. Crabapple is not permitted to draw guards' faces or the presence of security cameras. There is one angle you can stand at to take pictures of the overall site. There is a classification system that is, itself, classified.

In *Inside the Wire*, a documentary about GTMO produced for the DOD News Network, Air Force Sergeant Sean Lehman describes the system under which detainees live. 'The rules are prominently posted in several languages," he says, "and following them can mean getting such comfort items as playing cards, library books or even board games. It's a simple reward-based method that's explained to everyone held here.' Onscreen, Command Sergeant Major Anthony Menendez explains that the comfort items are made available or taken away 'according to a matrix' that defines the punishment by how detainees break the rules. This prevents guards from confiscating items arbitrarily, he says. Compliant prisoners are housed in different cellblocks and dressed differently from non-compliant prisoners. Compliant detainees wear tan or white, while non-compliant detainees wear orange. Standard operating procedures exist for all behaviours on the GTMO site, we are told by Brigadier General Jay Hood, ranging from visits with the Red Cross to how the detainee receives mail.

A section of the documentary is devoted to the importance of discipline – not on the part of the prisoners, but on the part of the guards, who must maintain a professional composure in the face of mistreatment by detainees. There is also discussion of the external oversight imposed by politicians, journalists and NGOs, who inspect the facility to ensure everything is kept compliant with international law. It sounds awfully panoptic.

Earlier in the documentary, Sergeant Lehman stands in the abandoned Camp X-Ray, which is overrun with weeds. Camp X-Ray was a makeshift camp in use from January to April 2002. If you associate GTMO with hooded figures kneeling inside chain-link cages, you are thinking of Camp X-Ray. U.S. forces complain that the press still assumes that GTMO and Camp X-Ray are synonymous. In the documentary, Sergeant Lehman describes the transition from Camp X-Ray to Camp Delta as being 'from makeshift to modern.' The much-maligned cages were temporary, he says: 'When I say temporary, I mean very temporary.'

X-Ray was housed in buildings that had been used in the 1990s as refugee shelters for Haitians displaced by the 1991 military coup d'état in their country. Cubans also began to attempt to cross into the U.S. military base after the sudden collapse of the Soviet Union and the loss of that country's subsidies. To do so, they had to cross a fifteen-kilometre stretch of the Cactus Curtain, a line of Nopalea cacti planted by Castro's troops in the early 1960s and fortified by minefields on both sides of that living border. Those who succeeded in making it through the treacherous obstacles were subsequently detained in Guantanamo's camps before the Americans sent them back to Cuba.

When the U.S. began to hold alleged combatants captured during the War on Terror, Camp X-Ray was pressed into service once again. A U.S. Department of Defense article from January 15, 2002, reported that fifty detainees were held at X-Ray, with more to come. The camp itself remained spartan during its brief period of use. each cellblock had a concrete floor, no plumbing, wire walls and a corrugated tin roof. The cells were open to the elements. Camp X Ray was dogged with torture allegations from the beginning of its reopening. Accusations became so onerous that reporters who wanted to visit the site were made to sign a set of rules that included: 'Asking questions or perspectives about ongoing and/or future operations or investigations can result in restricted access on Gitmo, removal from the installation, and/or revocation of DOD press credentials.'

Construction on Camp Delta – the 'modern' to X-Ray's 'makeshift' – began early in 2002. Delta is divided into several sub-camps, numbered according to construction date. The first camps were made from intermodal shipping containers, those ubiquitous remainders from the globalization of manufacturing. In North America, where many goods are shipped in but few are made, empty containers pile up, and architects requiring cheap and versatile materials sometimes turn to them. Sustainability advocates have built pop-up shops, homes, bars and LEED-certified pizza joints out of shipping containers. At GTMO, five cells were carved out of each twelve-metre container. Eight containers made a cellblock. *Inside the Wire* defines Camp Delta as a new kind of space, where prisoners' religious, psychiatric and dietary needs are minutely catered to. A civilized space.

Digital architecture and surveillance library Cryptome has collected and published documents that suggest that Camp 6, a cellblock in Camp Delta, was designed by American prison design firm SchenkelShultz. The firm runs a brisk trade in correctional facilities, municipal government buildings, airports and schools. In *Panopticon*, Bentham suggests that the design he proposes would be useful not only for prisons but also 'houses of industry, work-houses, poor-houses, lazarettos, manufactories, hospitals, mad-houses, and schools.' Camp Delta is not listed among the facilities in SchenkelShultz's portfolio, but according to Cryptome's research, Camp 6 most resembles U.S. Penitentiary, Terre Haute, in Indiana. Here is how the SchenkelShultz portfolio describes that facility: 'The United States Penitentiary is a maximum security prison and is also the first Federal Prison to incorporate a four-story special housing unit/special confinement unit to hold disciplinary, death row and administrative segregation inmates.' Some of Terre Haute's inmates work for UNICOR. Oklahoma City bomber Timothy McVeigh was executed there.

Through Foucauldian eyes, the story the U.S. military wants to tell about GTMO seems to repeat the juridical transition of 1757 to 1837. The parallels are clear: the *ancien régime*'s torturous execution with the torturous GTMO of old; the highly disciplined 'House of young prisoners in Paris' with the minutely managed GTMO of today. But where those parallels diverge is equally instructive.

First, the complete rupture between the old and new camps implied by the Pentagon documentary is misleading. The closure of X-Ray does not coincide with an end to torture allegations. Bradbury's memo authorizing waterboarding was written in 2005, long after the opening of Camp Delta. As recently as 2013, the Institute on Medicine as a Profession reported that its panel of medical, military, ethics and legal experts had determined that the doctors and psychologists working with detainees at GTMO were required by the DOD and CIA to contravene the rules of medical ethics.

More importantly for our purposes, the penal style of the *ancien régime* depended on a public spectacle. The procedures conducted at GTMO were done in secret.

'Among so many changes, I shall consider one: the disappearance of torture as a public spectacle,' writes Foucault. 'Today we are rather inclined to ignore it; perhaps, in its time, it gave rise to too much inflated rhetoric; perhaps it has been attributed too readily and too emphatically to a process of "humanization," thus dispensing with the need for further analysis... And yet the fact remains that a few decades saw the disappearance of the tortured, dismembered, amputated body, symbolically branded on face or shoulder, exposed alive or dead to public view. The body as the major target of penal repression disappeared.'

The shift, Foucault says, had to do with growing concerns that the spectacle of the execution — intended to reinforce the power of the sovereign through its very public reminder that the bodies of its subjects were subject to its every whim — had a tendency to inflame other passions in the spectators. Sometimes they might cheer for or sympathize with the condemned. Sometimes the condemned man or woman, with nothing left to lose, might be moved to sow further sedition in their final hours. Sometimes the mob turned on the magistrates and executioners and rescued the convict. The scaffold became seen as a place as liable to produce a folk hero as to reinforce the authority of the king. Similar fears have been expressed about the release of information relating to the treatment of DOD and CIA detainees. Al Qaeda's English-language recruitment magazine, *Inspire*, regularly refers to conditions at GTMO, including Osama bin Laden's editorial in the first issue in 2010, which references 'the crimes at Abu Ghraib and Guantanamo, those ugly crimes which shook the conscience of humanity.'

Guantanamo Bay was chosen as a detention site in order to construct a space outside of U.S. jurisdiction (as determined by the Bush-era Department of Justice). They needed a space where detainees determined to be dangerous could be held without charges. This should not be mistaken for a space outside of disciplinary power. 'Discipline sometimes requires *enclosure*,' writes Foucault, 'the specification of a place hetero-geneous to all others and closed in upon itself. It is the protected space of disciplinary monotony.'

The procedures approved by administration members like Yoo and Bradbury were not punishments. This is important. They were means of extracting information. Today, unlike the public executions of the *ancien régime*, the enhanced interro-gations are not treated as right and just actions, but as aberra-tions, shameful errors, necessary evils or overblown complaints.

Because of the complex legal arguments around the status of Camp Delta's detainees, GTMO has become a complex space. It houses people convicted of war crimes, people awaiting trial and people who will never be tried. Of the people who will never be tried, some have been cleared for release and not released. Others may never be cleared. In a dark illustration of the importance of legibility over justice to disciplinary systems, some of the convicted prisoners' sentences will end while detainees with less clear statuses remain confined.

And while Sergeant Lehman works hard to put Camp X-Ray in the past, it is worth remembering what was being said about it when it was open. On January 22, 2002, Secretary of Defense Donald Rumsfeld held a press conference to address already-circulating allegations of mistreatment and torture. There was no basis for them, he said. 'Just for the sake of the listening world, Guantanamo Bay's climate is different than Afghanistan. To be in an eight-by-eight cell in beautiful, sunny Guantanamo Bay, Cuba, is not a – inhumane treatment. And it has a roof.'

'Another advantage, still operating to the same ends, is the great load of trouble and disgust which it takes off the shoulders of those occasional inspectors of a higher order, such as *judges* and other *magistrates*, who, called down to this irksome task from the superior ranks of life, cannot but feel a proportionable repugnance to the discharge of it. Think how it is with them upon the present plans, and how it still must be upon the best plans that have been hitherto devised! The cells or apartments, however constructed, must, if there be nine hundred of them (as there were to have been upon the penitentiary-house plan,) be opened to the visitors, one by one. To do their business to any purpose, they must approach near to, and come almost in contact with each inhabitant; whose situation being watched over according to no other than the loose methods of inspection at present practicable, will on that account require the more minute and troublesome investigation on the part of these occasional superintendents. By this new plan, the disgust is entirely removed, and the trouble of going into such a room as the lodge, is no more than the trouble of going into any other.'

— Jeremy Bentham, *Panopticon; or,*
The Inspection-House

'And this illegality, while resented by the bourgeoisie where the ownership of land was concerned, was intolerable in commercial and industrial ownership: the development of the ports, the appearance of great warehouses in which merchandise was stored, the organization of huge workshops (with considerable quantities of raw materials, tools and manufactured articles, which belonged to the entrepreneurs and which were difficult to supervise) also necessitated a severe repression of illegality.'

— Michel Foucault, *Discipline & Punish*

After the planes hit the World Trade Center and the Pentagon, America seized up. Commercial flights were grounded, stranding passengers around the world. Landmarks and monuments all around the country were shut down. Border crossings of all kinds came under heavy scrutiny. The New York–based stock exchanges closed, remaining so until six days after the attack. The physical crisis and terrible toll of the attacks was met with a corresponding economic crisis – remember Bush's (apocryphal) exhortation to the citizenry to go shopping?

Speaking at the Ira M. Belfer Lecture at the Brooklyn Law School in 2011, Alan Bersin, Chief Diplomatic Officer for the Department of Homeland Security, looked back on the havoc:

> The resulting sense of insecurity stemmed from the fact that our borders had been violated. The reflexive response was to hunker down behind traditional concepts of borders as lines of defense. All planes were grounded and our maritime as well as aviation borders were closed in the immediate aftermath of 9/11. Similarly, our land borders virtually shut down as each entering vehicle from Mexico and Canada was inspected thoroughly.

The seizure was the result of a desperate attempt to understand where the attackers had come from and whether they could strike again. Wild rumours of secret invasions from Canada, cabals of sleeper agents and further strikes swept the nation. In its panic, the U.S. declared a War on Terror that turned out to mean invading a pair of countries, running a network of extrajudicial detainment facilities, assembling the

Wall Street

America's sprawling financial empire's metonymous name is Wall Street.

Wall Street probably takes its name from once being the northern edge of New Amsterdam, which was founded on the lower tip of Manhattan Island. In 1711, Wall Street was the location of New York's first official slave market. In 1789, it was the scene of the first U.S. presidential inauguration, and, in 1792, what would become the New York Stock Exchange was founded there. The Civil War and the resulting economic boom for the northern Union states cemented New York's status as financial centre.

world's most sprawling surveillance infrastructure and completely reconfiguring the departments responsible for monitoring the flows of goods and people across the border.

The 9/11 attacks targeted symbolic architecture: the Pentagon for the American military, the White House or Capitol for the American government and the WTC for the American economy – the twin towers had long stood in for America's vast financial system, whose centre is unquestionably New York. New York owes its position as a financial giant in large part to its origins as a port city.

Port

Port Newark is about twenty kilometres from the WTC site. It sits at the eastern edge of a stretch of industrialized former wetlands that include the port, an airport and a whole lot of petrochemical facilities. Every time newspapers write about the area, they quote a report by a former Coast Guard official who calls it 'the most dangerous two miles in America' – a temptation for terrorists.

If it were ever to be emptied, the 259-acre site would appear to be a giant parking lot protected by chain-link fences on the land side and ringed by tower cranes on the water side, with a collection of warehouses and administrative buildings in the middle. But it is never empty. The dominant form of the terminal is stacks of intermodal shipping containers, painted in muted oranges, reds, yellows, greens, whites, blues and browns.

Port Newark is part of a larger complex of terminals scattered around the New York–New Jersey Harbor Estuary. The estuary is a complicated space, lying at the confluence of the Atlantic Ocean, the Long Island Sound and the freshwater Hudson River. Left to its own devices, the estuary would be a broad silted expanse, with wetlands easing into the muddy shallows. Although the basic shape of the area remains the same, no part of the harbour has been unaffected by human intervention. As settlement expanded, the edges between terrain and water have been hardened: either built up to offer dry land for construction or deepened to offer better navigation for ships. This process began for Port Newark in 1910 with an angled shipping channel dug out on the northeastern quadrant of the wetlands. Construction accelerated during World War I, and then shipping languished, so Newark built an airport. By 1948, the Port Authority of New York and New Jersey had taken over both and begun modernization of the much-expanded facilities.

Shop for Freedom

It is a pervasive political myth that George W. Bush asked Americans to engage in mindless consumerism in the defence of freedom after September 11, 2001. Bush never directly asked Americans to go to the mall. On September 20, 2001, he did ask for 'continued participation and confidence in the American economy.' Writing for *Time*, Frank Pellegrini offered his own translation: 'And for God's sake keep shopping.'

In 1948, the dominant piers of the New York/New Jersey harbour were located in Manhattan and Brooklyn. This was a plainly insane arrangement – railroads needed to float cars across the river and trucks needed to fight their way through downtown traffic – but so much of New York's economy depended on the waterfront, either through direct employment or semi-direct effects like factories setting up shop upriver to be nearby, that the city fought hard to keep shipping where it was. Understanding how the harbour lost its place requires some history.

Docks

In *Discipline & Punish*, Foucault mentions ports as a specimen of the transition from the *ancien régime* to disciplinary society:

> Roughly speaking, one might say that, under the *Ancien Régime* each of the different social strata had its margin of tolerated illegality: the non-application of the rule, the non-observance of the innumerable edicts or ordinances were a condition of the political and economic functioning of society. This feature may not have been peculiar to the *Ancien Régime*. But illegality was so deeply rooted and so necessary to the life of each social stratum, that it had in a sense its own coherence and economy.

In the *ancien régime*, the collection of rules, offices, spheres of power and laws were often in conflict with one another, leaving a lot of room to manoeuvre:

> The least-favoured strata of the population did not have, in principle, any privileges: but they benefited, within the margins of what was imposed on them by law and custom, from a space of tolerance, gained by force or obstinacy; and this space was for them so indispensable a condition of existence that they were often

ready to rise up to defend it; the attempts that were made periodically to reduce it, by reviving old laws or by improving the methods of apprehending, provoked popular disturbances, just as attempts to reduce certain privileges disturbed the nobility, the clergy and the bourgeoisie.

But as the power of the sovereign waned and that of the bourgeoisie waxed, the tolerances changed. Bourgeois interests were more concerned with property crime. Practices like gathering firewood from the lands of nobility were now transformed from tolerated behaviour to property theft. Foucault writes:

> And this illegality, while resented by the bourgeoisie where the ownership of land was concerned, was intolerable in commercial and industrial ownership: the development of the ports, the appearance of great warehouses in which merchandise was stored, the organization of huge workshops (with considerable quantities of raw materials, tools and manufactured articles, which belonged to the entrepreneurs and which were difficult to supervise) also necessitated a severe repression of illegality.

The docks in particular were rife with petty corruption, smuggling and theft. Foucault quotes Patrick Colquhoun, the founder of the Thames River Police, who, in 1797, suggested that £250,000 of products from America and £500,000 of goods overall were stolen annually in the Port of London. Colquhoun estimated that a third of the 33,000 people employed on London's docks were known criminals and that all of the trades were 'on the game.'

The Thames River Police began as a one-year experiment to curb those losses, a project not without controversy. In its early days, a riotous mob of two thousand people rose up to defend their (illegal) livelihoods, threatening to burn down the River Police offices. In the end, the project was deemed a success. An interim report crowed that the patrols had cost a mere £4,200 and had saved £122,000 worth of cargo. In 1800, the British Parliament passed the Marine Police Bill, and the River Police were made permanent as they passed into public hands.

Colquhoun chronicled his experiences in his book *The Commerce and Policing of the River Thames*. It's said to have inspired the creation of similar police forces in Dublin, Sydney and New York City, and led to the establishment of preventative policing all over.

The Official Seal of the Department of Homeland Security

The seal of the Department of Homeland Security includes twenty-two stars, representing the twenty-two government entities that fell under its jurisdiction when it was created in 2002. For our purposes, the three most notable stars belong to the entities that were merged to form the new U.S. Customs and Border Protection, now the largest federal law enforcement agency in the U.S. Prior to the creation of the DHS, controlling the flow of people had been the purview of the Department of Justice, plants or animals the purview of the Department of Agriculture, and cargo or goods the purview of Department of the Treasury.

After the DHS merger, its chief diplomatic officer, Alan Bersin, envisioned a much more harmonious security approach and the invention of a new way of understanding national borders:

A unified border management was created for the first time in American history; and, it happens, for the first time across the globe in the world's history. Immigration, customs, and agricultural inspection authorities exercised by the same officer working for a single

In both 1797 and 1948 there were two main kinds of shipped goods. *Bulk* goods, like grain or oil, are essentially liquids that can be poured into a vessel. *Break bulk* goods are individually packaged in crates, barrels or bags that must be loaded individually. Successfully loading a ship with break bulk cargo is heavy manual labour that demands serious problem-solving in terms of cramming irregular objects into an irregularly shaped hold, while keeping an eye to the stability of the vessel. Managing all of that requires transportation networks to get the goods to the docks, people to unload arriving trains and trucks, a warehouse to store goods recently

agency defined by an overarching security mission, invented the institution of joint border management and the science and art of modern border protection.

However, unity is not the only concept portrayed in the seal. The eagle (because what kind of U.S. seal *doesn't* have an eagle on it, right?) at the centre of the seal has outstretched wings, which break through the inner circle to the outside. This is to represent how the DHS will eschew bureaucracy and 'perform government functions differently.' Reports of mismanagement, lack of oversight and consistently low employee morale have followed the agency since its creation. The *Washington Post* reported in 2008 that in its first five years, the DHS had overseen $15 billion in failed contracts, for (among other things) FEMA trailers, costly sensor systems that didn't work and Coast Guard ships that were built and subsequently scrapped.

The DHS can't be accused of having a sense of humour about itself, either. In 2011, it sent a cease-and-desist order to a seller on custom T-shirt site Zazzle who had made a version of the seal featuring a drunk eagle with the banner 'Department of Homeland Stupidity.' In February 2014, the DHS settled with the seller.

arrived or awaiting departure, and more people to get things from the warehouse to the ships. At every level – from pocketing goods that spill out of accidentally opened crates to misdirecting entire shipments – it's a system that offers a lot of opportunity for corruption, and New York's harbourfront was awash in it.

Here's how the Waterfront Commission of New York Harbor's history page characterizes those dark and dangerous days. It's enough to make Colquhoun despair.

In the early 1950's, an aging freighter, its belly loaded with crates, cartons, barrels and drums, is docked alongside one of the many ancient finger piers jutting into the waters of the Port of New York–New Jersey. At the sound of a whistle blown by a hiring foreman, a semi-circle of apprehensive longshoremen gathers in the hope that they will be selected to unload the vessel.

The foreman, often an ex-felon with a long criminal record, chooses laborers who are willing to 'kickback' a portion of their wages for the opportunity to unload the ship, piece by piece. Each hapless dockworker must subject himself to this notorious daily 'shape-up' to attain even the possibility of employment. The union, dominated by racketeers and criminals, does little to ease the burden of the rank-and-file worker.

Elsewhere on the pier lurk the loansharks, all too willing to 'assist' the underpaid longshoreman in feeding his family or in supporting his vices. The inability to repay these usurious loans results in violent consequences for the longshoreman-borrower. Bookmaking on the pier increases business for the loansharks.

Cargo theft and pilferage are rampant. Pier guards are unwilling or unable to contain thievery.

At the foot of the pier, a parasitic 'public loader' coerces truckers to employ him to unload and load trucks, even though the 'services' of these loaders are not needed or wanted.

In a downtown restaurant, an officer of a stevedoring firm pays a 'gratuity' to a waterfront union official to insure 'labor peace.' 'Quickie' strikes are commonplace. The stevedore company official gladly bribes an executive of a steamship company for a lucrative contract.

For shippers, corruption was just one of several problems with doing business on New York's waterfront. Sending goods via New York's port meant: trucks contending with Manhattan traffic or train cars being floated across the river; gangs that insisted on a monopoly on unloading trucks; labour disruptions, wildcat strikes and clashes between rival unions; and mob corruption. This all took place atop piers that were nearly a century old, in poor repair and ill-suited for mechanized shipping. Still, in 1944, New York handled one-third of all U.S. waterborne exports. By the time the WTC towers fell, however, the vast majority of that traffic had moved to New Jersey and the rest to Brooklyn. Manhattan was handling no shipping traffic at all.

Containers

If you wanted to pick a moment to herald that shift, you could do worse than April 26, 1956. That's the day the SS *Ideal X* left from Port Newark, bound for Houston, Texas, with a cargo of fifty-eight shipping containers. In Houston, fifty-eight flatbed trucks were waiting to accept those loads. Instead of hundreds or thousands of individual items being packed and unpacked on the dock, unloading the SS *Ideal X* required only fifty-eight moves. A lot of things happened between then and now, but the result was a global shipping industry reliant on standardized and interchangeable metal boxes that dramatically dropped the cost of loading and unloading, and so the costs of shipping overall. Today, there are two main kinds of shipping: *bulk* and *containerized*. Break bulk still happens, but it is rare.

The advent of standardized container shipping caused ripple effects around the globe, making changes in worldwide patterns of manufacturing and production, and introducing the 'just in time' product delivery strategy. With reliable international shipping, coordinated down to the minute with rail and truck delivery, it is now easier for companies to order exactly what they need when they need it, rather than holding inventory in warehouses until required.

The switch to containers also meant that the physical shape of the world's port areas changed dramatically. In the pre-container days, ports needed long piers, where ships could tie up for the extended process of packing and unpacking cargo. In the container era, those piers are no longer as necessary. Instead, you need a huge amount of space to store the containers as they come off the ships. These space requirements meant that ports in heavily urbanized areas like Manhattan could not handle the new type of shipping, and so Port Newark stepped into the breach. Manhattan's piers emptied out, abandoning the relatively well-paid labourers who had worked the docks. Lower Manhattan now belonged to the financial industry, rather than to trade itself.

Located next to a major rail line and the New Jersey Turnpike, Port Newark – with its vast, flat, filled-in marshland – was an ideal place to accommodate the rise of container shipping. Today, together with the Elizabeth–Port Authority Marine Terminal, the Howland Hook Marine Terminal, the Brooklyn–Port Authority Marine Terminal, the Red Hook Container Terminal and the Port Jersey Port Authority Marine Terminal, it forms the Port of New York and New Jersey, the largest container port in the eastern United States. (The Port Authority also owns the WTC site.)

One of the hopes of containerization was that it would break the hold of organized crime and general criminality on the docks. It is much harder to pilfer from a sealed thirty-ton container than to grab a few bottles of rum from an open crate. But organized crime is nothing if not adaptable, and the State of New Jersey Commission of Investigation's annual reports say that the Genovese crime family maintains a strong hold on New Jersey's dockyards to this day

When containers came in, one of the groups who protested the most were dockworker unions. The bulk of their work came from those lengthy loading and unloading jobs, which were about to disappear. When the cargo is contained in boxes and unloaded with cranes, far fewer workers are required. At their height, the longshoremen's unions had about forty thousand members. Today, that number is closer to four thousand. But fewer workers picking around the cargo doesn't necessarily mean less crime. It just means different crime.

The accumulation of cargo means that crime increases in scale. Containers make certain kinds of pilfering harder, but open up new avenues for smuggling and wholesale theft. Theft-wise, now you're not just dealing with someone who can make off with a single crate, but someone with the resources to take an entire container, or even a whole shipment. Sealing up the cargo in containers opens up other avenues of deception. There's a new obscurity created by putting stuff in boxes and, to make matters worse, shippers routinely lie about the contents even when they don't contain contraband. In many cases, mobsters have moved outward to prey on container logistics, with mob-run repair shops and other businesses servicing the supply chain.

And there is still plenty of opportunity for corruption with the unions. In 2007, the Inspector General of New York began an investigation into the Waterfront Commission. The resulting 2009 report detailed a cartoonish level of malfeasance, ranging from on-duty officers being detailed to guard their bosses' empty parking spots to the commission failing to enforce regulations that prevent people with racketeering convictions from holding offices in the dockworker unions. A 2012 report issued by the newly reformed Waterfront Commission documented union positions filled by relatives of organized-crime figures, including nine relatives of Vincent 'the Oddfather' Gigante, three of whom earned $400,000 a year as shop stewards. Despite the problems, the New York/New Jersey port remains the country's seventh largest by tons and the second largest by value (after Houston). Just as in the 1700s, certain kinds of illegalities are tolerated, while others are heavily constrained.

Terror

Contemporary port security has its own clear origin myth. There was a previous regime, then there was September 11, and now everything has changed. The fall of the towers haunts every related position paper, treaty and study. No description of port security or contemporary customs practices can help but mention it, drawing from a glossary of metonymy and euphemism: the attacks, the events, the strategic incident, the tragedy.

Whatever the name, the clear narrative is that the security regime in place is a child of that terrible, fateful day. The change didn't happen all at once. It has been built up over a decade as a patchwork of internal laws, regulations and international treaties: the Maritime Transportation Security Act; the Container Security Initiative; Customs–Trade Partnership Against Terrorism; the International Ship and Port Facility Security Code; the GreenLane Maritime Cargo Security Act; the Framework of Standards to Secure and Facilitate Trade (SAFE); the Secure Freight Initiative. Customs and security officials make it clear that the work is ongoing, in a permanent state of refinement and increasing discipline.

The container plays a starring role in these fears as the source of insecurity. Writing for the *World Customs Journal*, David Hesketh, a senior manager with HM Revenue and Customs in the U.K., tells an appealing just-so story of the time before containerization and the need for the new regimes.

> From its beginnings the international trade process was relatively straightforward. The buyer would board a ship and travel to another country, identify the goods they wanted, pay for them, return to the ship, load the goods, return to their own country aboard the ship with their goods, unload them, pay the customs duty and sell them at the market. However, when the buyer stopped travelling to buy the goods and stopped the face-to-face transaction, international commerce and transport became more complicated. Communication became more difficult. Trust and agreements were replaced by contracts, jurisdictions, different currencies and systems of payment and different languages, ships, containers and people. These continually change.

Hesketh is not clear on when he thinks the 'relatively straightforward' period ended, and we are being a little unfair by introducing him right after the section where we detail the long and entrenched history of crime on the docks. His implication is that the fact of nothing getting inspected is a recent development, a kind of degenerate contemporary era where too-rapid transit, too many agents and too much cargo have broken down chains of custody and evidence. Hesketh's evoked golden era never existed, but he is right that the complex networks of supply make the current condition particularly opaque.

With the spectre of terrorism, the balance of tolerance for illegalities and irregularities has shifted again. As America sought to gain control of the borders, particular concern was paid to the shipping industry as a vector of threat. The fear is that the sheer volume of physical goods entering the U.S. via containers makes ports an extremely tempting target for the economic havoc that an attack would cause. Meanwhile, the incredible volume of goods entering the U.S. via containers and freight makes inspecting them all essentially impossible. The thing that makes blowing up a port tempting is the very thing that makes blowing up a port possible.

After all, part of the great terror of September 11 was that al Qaeda had turned civilian infrastructure against the U.S. Using civilian box cutters, they took control of civilian aircraft. Using skills learned at a civil aviation school, they turned those planes into tower-toppling missiles.

You can pack a lot of mayhem into an 8 x 8.5 x 40-foot space with a 26.6-ton capacity. Evidence submitted to a 2005 hearing before the Subcommittee on Prevention of Nuclear and Biological Attack warned that it was just a matter of time before an adversary attempted a nuclear attack. The paper, which argues for an offshore detection system, worries that cargo ships could become a 'Poor Man's ICBM [Intercontinental Ballistic Missile].' The nightmare scenario is that a container with a nuclear weapon in it simply sails into an American port, and then explodes while awaiting inspection.

No doubt, the case of Uzair Paracha loomed over those hearings. In 2003, Paracha was sentenced to thirty years for trying to make it look like Majid Khan (now serving time at GTMO as a high-value detainee) was living in the U.S. Paracha's own father, Saifullah Paracha, is also currently being held without charge at GTMO. The Parachas ran an import business, bringing clothes to the U.S. and selling them to Kmart. During interrogation, accused September 11th architect Khalid Sheikh Mohammed reportedly talked about his interest in using the Parachas' shipping containers to smuggle explosives.

For the shipping industry, the situation is more complicated. Sure, terrorism is a threat to the movement of their goods along the supply chain, but so are security checkpoints. Manufacturing parts in one country, assembling them into finished commodities in another and selling them in a third requires the smooth, unimpeded movement of those goods around the world. National borders can get in the way of that smooth movement.

From a logistics perspective, terror attacks, overly strict security, piracy, shipwrecks, bad weather, labour disruptions and incompetent captains are all of a kind. For manufacturers and their retail clients, a perfectly legitimate customs delay and a terrorist attack are basically indistinguishable. In both cases, they slow down the flow of goods. The Poor Man's ICBM is one nightmare scenario. The other nightmare scenario is a system so thoroughly designed to prevent attacks that the delays it causes are tantamount to an attack happening.

Toronto-based geographer Deborah Cowen traces the history of the modern supply chain to the logistical challenges of World War II, the industrial war. A good portion of the work in that conflict involved moving a great number of people and manufactured goods to foreign places. After the war, Cowen says, men with new experience and methods for understanding the mass movement of goods transitioned into business and applied those skills to the globalization of manufacturing.

Military logistics has never been particularly concerned with national borders (indeed, when your army is involved in a heavy logistical operation, it generally involves violating *someone's* borders). Instead, it tends to be more concerned with the discipline and protection of its own chain. Generally speaking, the security concerns of a multinational manufacturing chain are the same. National borders are one of many regulatory and geographical obstacles to overcome, and the discipline of logistics is about shaving off delays and finding new efficiencies to drop the cost of moving goods as much as possible.

This results in some powerfully strange conceptual models. In a 2005 Congressional Services Research report, *Port and Maritime Security: Background and Issues for Congress*, the author attempts to quantify the potential harms of a terrorist action in terms of the economic cost of a recent labour dispute on the west coast.

What this means for the port is that it is a site of two overlapping but not entirely congruous disciplinary regimes. The State and the company agree that the contents should not be pilfered by unauthorized persons. But the State wants to be certain there are no weapons or contraband inside the container and the company wants the container to get to its destination unimpeded. The State is in some agreement with this because the container represents economic benefits, and at the same time pleads with the company to accept some reasonable security precautions on the grounds that a successful terrorist attack would cause some *serious* delays.

Here is how *Port and Maritime Security: Background and Issues for Congress* sells the advantages of security via side benefits:

> Many experts see economic benefits to tighter control over maritime commerce. Resources put towards seaport security can also reduce cargo theft, narcotic and migrant smuggling, trade law violations, the accidental introduction of invasive species, and the cost of cargo insurance. Improved planning for responding to a terrorist attack at a seaport could also improve responses to other emergencies, such as natural disasters or transportation accidents. New technologies intended to convert the sea container into a 'smart box,' such as electronic seals, sensors, or tracking devices,

could also improve shipment integrity, help carriers improve their equipment utilization, and help cargo owners track their shipments.

It's an uphill battle, the report notes, because so many people are involved in the packing process.

The parties involved in a shipment usually include the exporter, the importer, a freight forwarder, a customs broker, a customs inspector, inland transportation provider(s) (which may include more than one trucker or railroad), the port operators, possibly a feeder ship, and the ocean carrier. Each transfer of the container from one party to the next is a point of vulnerability in the supply chain.

Even worse, the conflicting interests of all these different parties mean that shippers routinely lie about the contents. Writing for the *World Customs Journal*, Hesketh explains:

If the shipper declares the true value of the goods to the carrier then the freight rates increase significantly because the carrier is then liable for the entire cost in the event of damage or loss. So the shipper reduces the description of the goods and omits the true value on the bill of lading then takes out separate insurance to cover the risk.

The interest for shippers is to have a supply chain that is transparent to themselves but opaque to outsiders, including the people carrying their goods.

Borders

The port also causes serious problems for the interrelated security regimes of the State. Most countries rely on a strict division of domestic and foreign jurisdictions for organizing their police and military security. For this to work, countries must have a well-defined inside and outside. The border is a place where people enjoy few rights, and the overlapping jurisdictions of law enforcement and the military lead to confusion about the nature of security breaches. If someone breaks into a port, is it a crime? A protest? An act of terror? An act of war? Each option results in different consequences for the actor and demands responses from different institutions, even though it's the same act. Cowen calls this zone of confused conditions 'the Seam.'

What's important to note is that the Seam is not necessarily co-extensive with the border. For instance, in the U.S. there are 'inland ports' in the middle of the continent that function effectively as border towns. To keep the supply chain running smoothly, cities like Dallas and Kansas City have customs offices where containers – still sealed from their overseas journeys – are accepted. Inspecting cargo inland takes some of the pressure off the ports, but it results in the weird situation of boxes travelling overland in the U.S. when they haven't been officially accepted into the country. In other places, the U.S. stations customs officials overseas to pre-clear goods or people before they even leave their origin country. The heightened regimes of border security reach far beyond the everyday, geographic border.

Because the Department of Homeland Security's goal is to keep dangerous goods and people away from the U.S., their approach is to extend the Seam overseas. This isn't a diagnosis on our part, this is literally what they say, in their own words. Here's the DHS's Bersin again:

> We began to understand that our borders begin not where our ports of entry are located, but rather, where passengers board air carriers and freight is loaded on maritime vessels bound for those ports of entry. In order to forge practical arrangements to take both travel and

trade security into account, borders needed to be viewed and managed as flows of people and goods as much as lines in the sand, on the water, or through the air.

There are various initiatives intended to bring order to the Seam. One of the first was the Container Security Initiative, launched in 2002. It put U.S. customs officers in foreign ports to inspect cargo bound for U.S. destinations. This is the clearest and most architectural instance of extending the borders – they moved the guard posts.

More interesting to us for its Foucauldian dimensions is the Customs–Trade Partnership Against Terrorism (C-TPAT), launched in 2001. It's an effort to bring the disciplinary needs of the importers in line with those of the State. The program is voluntary. Participant companies get security training and submit to inspections and audits to ensure their own supply chain is safe. The security training ostensibly offers benefits to the importers by reducing theft, but the program also offers 'green lanes' at customs and fewer inspections. It's similar to the NEXUS or SENTRI programs for 'trusted travellers' between the U.S. and Canada, and the U.S. and Mexico, respectively. The frequent flyer will go through a rigorous screening in exchange for quicker lineups and a more seamless experience at the border. This is a classic discipline arrangement. The more the traveller complies with the disciplinary regime, the better his experience becomes. With C-TPAT, the shipping companies themselves do the work of internalizing the security needs of the U.S.

That's the promise, anyway. Implementation has proven difficult, and in a 2008 report for the U.S. International Trade Commission, *The Post-9/11 Global Framework for Cargo Security*, analysts cautioned that the importers were complaining about the program: 'In particular, a 2007 study conducted by the University of Virginia found that whereas the annual costs to U.S. importers of participation in C-TPAT were more than

$30,000, the benefits of such participation, including increased supply chain security and fewer customs inspections, had not yet been fully realized.'

Last on our tour of troubled initiatives is the '100% scanning law.' The 9/11 Commission Recommendations Act of 2007 includes a mandate that 100 percent of all maritime cargo containers entering U.S. ports be scanned for radioactive material by 2012. To put that in perspective, in 2006 only about 4 percent of containers that made landfall in Port Newark were scanned, and a report penned by Rutgers University concluded that exceeding 7 percent would cause a massive spike in costs and time delays.

So far as we can tell, the worldwide shipping industry responded to the law by quietly freaking out and then simply refusing to implement it. In 2012, the number of pre-scanned containers held steady at 4 percent. Homeland Security Secretary Janet Napolitano granted a two-year waiver, but there was no sign that things would be any better in 2014.

Bentham could have warned Congress that 100 percent scanning was a bad plan. The whole point of the panoptic approach is that you don't need 100 percent observation – it's a bad use of resources. This is particularly true of detection technologies like the cargo scanners. Every time you run a scan, there is a small chance of a false positive (naturally radioactive materials like certain ceramics and kitty litter can trigger the detectors, the containers and their contents can scramble the signals, and it all happens in a generally chaotic environment). In the 2005 report *Evaluating the Viability of 100 Per Cent Container Inspection at America's Ports*, RAND Corporation researchers found that 5 percent of cargo containers were being scanned, and of those, 5 percent were flagged for physical examination. Physical examination meant unpacking and repacking the container, a process that could take fifteen to twenty inspectors four hours, or as long as three days for a team of five.

The Port of New York and New Jersey handled about 2.9 million containers in 2010, of which about 7,300 were flagged for physical inspection. Under 100 percent scanning, that would have been closer to 150,000 physical inspections, or hundreds of containers pulled aside each day. Industry and security advocates have accordingly proposed a far more panoptic alternative. Recognizing that you can't scan everything, they have emphasized using surveillance and collected data to work out which cans to scan.

Here's Bersin again, explaining the scope of the operation as far as data collection at Customs and Border Protection:

> To fulfill its mission CBP has developed the U.S. government's largest collection, storage, and dissemination functions with respect to unclassified data. On a typical day, CBP exchanges 1.35 billion electronic messages with other government agencies, transportation carriers, customs brokers, and the plethora of additional participants in global travel networks and supply chains.

And here is what they do with all that information:

> These analytical communications are managed by CBP's National Targeting Centers for Passengers and Cargo, located in Virginia. They permit access, respectively, to records of each traveler and every cargo shipment – land, sea, and air – that have crossed a U.S. border through a port of entry during the past eight years, legally or illegally. Sophisticated rule searches, utilizing complex algorithms, scan this data for both known and unknown threats based on potential risks identified by DHS and the intelligence community.

This is perfectly panoptic thinking. We don't look at every container, but we *could!* We have *powerful algorithms* that tell us when you are doing something untoward and we will find you.

Non-Human Agents Don't Care How Vigilant You Pretend to Be

In 2011, the Associated Press reported an unintended consequence of the War on Terror. In the rush to shore up the nation's borders against human threats, the merging of people, agricultural goods and cargo into a single agency had resulted in a de-emphasis on the agricultural inspections:

> Using the Freedom of Information Act, the AP obtained data on border inspections covering the period from 2001 to 2010. The analysis showed that the number of inspections, along with the number of foreign species that were stopped, fell dramatically in the years after the Homeland Security Department was formed. During much of the same period, the number of crop-threatening pests that got into the U.S spiked, from eight in 1999 to at least thirty in 2010.

> The report goes on to list a series of specific outbreaks, noting that 'in all, the number of pest cases intercepted at U.S. ports of entry fell from more than 81,200 in 2002 to fewer than

But even as this power is being asserted, reasons for skepticism appear. Really? You mean to say you have a record of every illegal cargo shipment that passed through the ports? How did they make it through, then?

The ongoing influence of the Genovese family on Port Newark and the nearly complete failure of the Waterfront Commission to do its job suggest that reality is not quite as well-controlled as Bersin wants to assert. It also suggests a reason for skepticism in Bentham's faith in either the power of surveillance or in rational self-interest to prevent anti-social behaviour.

The presence of several different security agencies doesn't stop the mob. Instead, organized crime uses a mixture of low-

58,500 in 2006, before creeping back up in 2007, when the farm industry and members of Congress began complaining.'

The problems began when the Homeland Security Department absorbed inspectors who worked for the Department of Agriculture. The move put plant and insect scientists alongside gun-toting agents from Customs and Border Protection and resulted in a bitter culture clash.

Agriculture supervisors were replaced in the chain of command by officials unfamiliar with crop science. Hundreds of inspectors resigned, retired or transferred to other agencies. Some of the inspectors who remained on the job lost their offices and desks and were forced to work out of the trunks of their cars.

It took authorities years 'to learn there's an important mission there,' said Joe Cavey, head of pest identification for a USDA inspection service 'Yeah, maybe a radioactive bomb is more important, but you have to do both things.'

level operatives and a powerful disciplinary regime of its own (not least of which is a notorious code of silence) to test the limits of the security regime and take those liberties that Bentham feared. Some of the individuals may be caught, but it doesn't do much harm to the organization as a whole.

In his 'Docile Bodies' chapter, Foucault uses a port to illustrate the challenges to discipline and the distribution of individuals in space:

A port, and a military port is — with its circulation of goods, men signed up willingly or by force, sailors embarking and disembarking, diseases and epidemics

— a place of desertion, smuggling, contagion: it is a crossroads for dangerous mixtures, a meeting-place for forbidden circulations.

He notes here the same feeling of lawlessness and liminality that has always been associated with port zones. The particular port he's mentioning also had a naval hospital, so it was especially vital that they be able to contain any diseases that came through. The specialized spaces inside the hospital allow for control, since contagious patients can be isolated as needed. It is impossible to prevent outbreaks (be they of disease, labour strife or smuggling) unless proper discipline is maintained.

At Port Newark, the objects under disciplinary control are commodities, but here they are sick sailors. In the naval hospital, the number, location, medical issue and identity of each patient marked his hospital bed. Classification is a vital component to the disciplinary regimes Foucault describes, whether it's being applied to schoolchildren, prisoners or patients. At Newark, it is the containers that are marked, sealed so that tampering is obvious, and constantly monitored as they proceed around the world. Their handlers are marked too, by customs, by their employers, by their union, by their clients, by the mob and by al Qaeda. The shift to containerized shipping in places like Port Newark allowed for disciplined cargoes, but the system still isn't as perfect as the U.S. government would like it to be. Networks of discipline cooperate, conflict and compete with one another. Into this gap between the ideal and the real world fall all sorts of malfeasance. The port is still a liminal space.

An Incomplete Design History of the Jersey Barrier

When the U.S. interstate highway system was first conceived, each state took care of its own safety systems. It wasn't yet known what was going to work well, so trial-and-error was the order of the day. One of the major problems the states faced was reducing damage from accidents and out-of-control vehicles. Head-on collisions were the worst kind, so it was clear a median was needed between the opposing directions of fast-moving traffic. But what would it look like?

New Jersey's first design was a short barrier, about forty-five centimetres tall with angled curbs on either side. Crash statistics came in after they were installed – surprisingly, not before they were placed on highways – leading to a series of redesigns. The standard size now used is just over a metre tall, with a wide eighty-centimetre base and thirty centimetres at the top. The barrier is most recognizable for the kink in the slope of the sides. The particular angles of the slope are intended to deflect out-of-control vehicles, preventing them from flipping over while protecting the oncoming lane. But car design is not static, and so neither is the barrier's design. In the 1970s, when cars were larger, the break point of the slope was higher than it typically is now.

The modularity of Jersey barriers makes them well-suited to following the curving lines of freeways and easy to maintain – damaged sections can simply be removed and replaced. It also makes them well-suited to temporary installation. They are used to reroute traffic around construction or away from newly threatened urban spaces. In L.A., they are often seen around areas prone to erosion and mudslides.

After the WTC attacks, many U.S. embassies carved out a buffer zone for themselves with Jersey barriers. In the U.S. military, they are sometimes known as 'Qaddafi blocks,' after their use intensified around military installations following a series of truck-bomb attacks in Beirut in 1983. However, they're not really intended to stop vehicle-borne bombs. Your security consultant will definitely recommend switching to gates or bollards for your future security needs. Jersey barriers can only be a stop-gap.

In 2010, modified Jersey barriers were used to block off parts of Toronto for the G20 summit. They made a solid and unmovable base for the wire fencing that delineated the security perimeter around the downtown core of the city. The innovation was a response to previous anti-globalization protests, which had seen conventional security fences knocked over by protesters.

'It is obvious that, in all these instances, the more constantly the persons to be inspected are under the eyes of the persons who should inspect them, the more perfectly will the purpose of the establishment have been attained. Ideal perfection, if that were the object, would require that each person should actually be in that predicament, during every instant of time. This being impossible, the next thing to be wished for is, that, at every instant, seeing reason to believe as much, and not being able to satisfy himself to the contrary, he should *conceive* himself to be so.'

— Jeremy Bentham, *Panopticon; or,*
The Inspection-House

'In this central and centralized humanity, the effect and instrument of complex power relations, bodies and forces subjected by multiple mechanisms of "incarceration", objects for discourses that are themselves elements for this strategy, we must hear the distant roar of battle.'

— Michel Foucault, *Discipline & Punish*

London's Ring of Steel

Time was, there were thirty-eight different ways you could drive into the square mile that forms the City of London (located inside London, the metropolitan area). Starting in the 1990s, many of those roads were gradually shut to incoming traffic. These days, there are only sixteen ways to enter the financial heart of Britain by private vehicle.

The reason for this is Ireland. We will not attempt to explain the Troubles here, except to say they happened and there was a great deal of serious violence including more than a few bombings, and most of those bombings happened in Northern Ireland, but some happened in England. In response, cities began to fortify themselves.

Belfast, the capital of Northern Ireland, was the first city to fortify its central zone with high railings, and to restrict traffic to a few policed entrances. Beginning in the 1970s, police road checks became commonplace, with special attention paid to vans that were suspected of carrying bombs. By the 1990s, private vehicles were only rarely allowed into the city centre, and buses and pedestrians were routinely checked as well.

London's fortifications came later. The first physical barrier was erected in 1989, after an attempt on Prime Minister Margaret Thatcher's life. Wrought-iron gates were installed at both ends of the street leading to the prime minister's residence at 10 Downing Street, and the street was closed to the public. Tensions reached a fever pitch in the early 1990s as Thatcher's successor, John Major, would not enter talks with Irish republican political party Sinn Féin until the Provisional Irish Republican Army (PIRA or IRA) declared a ceasefire.

Threatened City

A word about political geography: the City of London is not to be confused with London. London is a sprawling megalopolis with a population of 8 to 21 million people, depending on how you count and where you draw the edges of the urban area. The City of London is London's ancient core, a 1.12-square-mile enclave defined by medieval borders, with a population of 7,375. It is the financial heart of England's economy and, for a long time, was the financial capital of the world. During the day, its population swells to about 300,000 people, mostly financial-services workers. Despite its age and the presence of iconic historical landmarks like St. Paul's Cathedral, bombing during World War II and development pressures have meant a lot of new construction. The skyline is dominated by many of the tallest skyscrapers in the U.K. During elections, the businesses that operate in the City are permitted to vote (votes are apportioned by a formula that results in about 32,000 non-resident voters – the City is the last place in the U.K. that allows businesses to vote). The City also has its own police force, independent of the Metropolitan Police Service, which polices the rest of London. From 1986 to 1993, leadership of the force fell to City of London police commissioner Owen Kelly.

Because of its economic importance, the City of London was a regular target for IRA attacks. In 1990, they bombed the London Stock Exchange. In 1992, the day after Major's Conservatives' victory in the general election, a bomb was set off outside the Baltic Exchange in St. Mary Axe, a City parish, killing three and injuring one hundred. The one-ton fertilizer bomb in the back of a truck caused £800 million in damage, £200 million more than all ten thousand previous Troubles-related bombings combined.

The St. Mary Axe incident prompted the City police force to introduce 'rolling random roadblocks.' Police intelligence developed a profile of what a terrorist vehicle might look like and roadblocks were set up to stop and search such vehicles before they came into the City. At the time, there were too many avenues leading into the area for all streets to be monitored, so the roadblocks were moved around from day to day. Speaking after his retirement, Kelly said that even if the police had had enough manpower to check every street, the Police and Criminal Evidence Act of 1984 and concerns about public opinion would have prevented them from doing so. For the first time in the U.K., the uniformed police performing those road checks were armed, since some unarmed officers had recently become IRA victims. CCTV cameras were already in place in the City for traffic management, and those were redeployed to focus on recording incoming traffic. The network of private, non-police-affiliated CCTV cameras also grew, as insurance companies encouraged businesses to cover their premises.

The problem was increasingly large vehicle-borne bombs. In Ireland, the IRA had attempted to remote-pilot an 8,000-pound bomb on a tractor-trailer into checkpoints, and on April 24, 1993, they detonated a one-ton truck bomb on Bishopsgate, a major road in London's financial district. Damages exceeded £350 million, forty people were injured and one was killed. The London mayor pleaded the City's case, telling Prime Minister Major that 'the City of London earned £17 billion last year for the nation as a whole. Its operating environment and future must be preserved.' The City was chosen for protection because of its economic importance for the nation, rather than more symbolic locations like the Houses of Parliament or Buckingham Palace, both of which lie outside the Square Mile. (It is hard to imagine a clearer illustration of the link between discipline and industrial commerce than a decision to protect the seat of finance over the throne.)

Police strategy was to restructure traffic flows into and out of the City, and augment that by a network of barriers and sentry boxes. In 1984, section 12 of the Road Traffic Management Act had granted the City of London police commissioner some powers over traffic, but it wasn't until the Bishopsgate bombing that Kelly really started flexing his muscles, developing what would become known as the Ring of Steel.

London's Ring of Steel takes its name from a comparable security project in Belfast and followed a similar approach – a radical retrofit of the urban environment focused on controlling vehicular traffic to ward off bombs. Kelly used his powers to shut down many routes into the City. Some streets were blocked off entirely while others were converted to outbound-only. A reduction of the streets leading in meant the police could concentrate on monitoring those that remained, using both officers and the already-omnipresent CCTV cameras.

To assist with monitoring, inbound roads were narrowed, and chicanes (sections with extra turns) were added. Both had the effect of slowing traffic, ensuring that security cameras could get a clear shot of drivers. Sentry boxes were installed in medians and prominently manned by police officers.

Restructured Space

Foucault talks about this kind of rearrangement of space in *Discipline & Punish*. He argues that disciplinary power imposes compulsory visibility on its subjects, while seeking to remain invisible itself. In the 'space of domination, disciplinary power manifests its potency, essentially, by arranging objects.' By rearranging the possible ways to enter the City of London, the police force demands that residents and visitors to the area make themselves more visible. Entry to the City is limited and monitored. People are encouraged to visit the area in order to participate in the mechanisms of capitalism, either by working in one of the many financial institutions or by spending money at retail shops. Other types of behaviour may be looked upon with suspicion.

After Kelly retired in December 1993, he took a moment to look back over the Ring of Steel initiative:

> It was probably the most contentious decision any police chief has had to take in recent times and I am pleased that so far I have been proved right. It may be that hand-held devices will still penetrate the cordon, but given this open and free society and the hundreds of thousands of people who enter the City every day in a variety of transport systems, there is no scheme which could prevent that. Certainly it is now much more difficult to bring in a large vehicle-borne bomb.

Let's interrupt Kelly here for a moment and return to Foucault. In the latter chapters of *Discipline & Punish*, he talks about how punitive disciplinary institutions formed a network in the eighteenth century. As people moved from the school to the hospital to the workhouse to the prison, they were never outside of the disciplinary regime. What Foucault called the 'carceral archipelago' translated the techniques of the prison into everyday life. It's exactly this type of widening self-justification that Kelly is describing. While public opinion held the police back after the St. Mary Axe bombing, another blast the following year was all the police needed to enforce measures that would have been considered 'draconian' in 1992. Back to Kelly:

> The benefits of the scheme are now widely acknowledged. There have been no more vehicle-borne terrorist bombs, despite the threatening letters the PIRA sent to foreign banks. Crime generally in the City has reduced by 17 per cent, and this on a reduction of 10.6 per cent in 1992 that was a result of our extra activity after the St Mary Axe incident. Motor traffic is much reduced and flows more easily. Pedestrians can move around in greater safety and all pollution levels have dropped measurably.

There is an element of theatricality to the Ring of Steel. In its early days, it consisted of a visible police presence, temporary barriers and traffic cones (some residents derisively called it the 'Ring of Plastic'). The visible presence of police was a key component both in terms of warning off terrorists and reassuring locals. Reducing the number of entry points also served a human-resources purpose in the Ring of Plastic days; the fewer entrances there were, the fewer the officers required to patrol them. The Ring of Steel expanded the perception of protection provided by the Downing Street gates all around the City of London, providing the same refuge for the financial centre as for the nation's political leaders.

Over time, the plastic was replaced with concrete as the new regime accreted permanence. Bright plastic traffic cones have been replaced with more subtle measures: sidewalks and buildings block streets, bollards spring up on roadsides, trees and concrete planters appear, and CCTV cameras monitor the remaining entryways. After the IRA ceasefires in 1994 and 1997, security was relaxed. Today, the public police presence has largely fallen away, leaving the permanent changes to the area's architecture, as well as the cameras. The idea is to balance security with paranoia, to ensure that the populace isn't constantly preoccupied with worry about terrorist threats.

Since September 11, 2001, counterterrorism measures have waxed and waned as a priority in the city. In the early 2000s, 1,500 extra police officers were deployed around London, both in the City and in other areas. Gradually, the City's Ring of Steel has been expanded and reproduced to protect other sites of economic or symbolic importance around other nearby areas of London, including Smithfield and the Barbican Centre. Even when the threat level remains low, the permanent architectural changes wrought by the various iterations of the Ring remain.

We are writing about the Ring of Steel because *Discipline & Punish* climaxes with an image of the carceral city. Having begun with the *ancien régime* of spectacular torture, and moved through the Enlightenment ideals of better behaviour through architecture, Foucault spends much of the text on the question of prisons, their origin, their contemporary use and their panop tic design. He begins showing panoptic technology everywhere: in hospitals, in factories, in military encampments and in schools. Finally, Foucault comes to society as a whole, quoting an extensive passage from an anonymous correspondent to the political paper *La Phalange*, written in 1836:

Moralists, philosophers, legislators, flatterers of civiliza- tion, this is the plan of your Paris, neatly ordered and arranged, here is the improved plan in which all like things are gathered together. At the centre, and within a first enclosure: hospitals for all diseases, almshouses for all types of poverty, madhouses, prisons, convict- prisons for men, women and children. Around the first enclosure, barracks, courtrooms, police stations, houses for prison warders, scaffolds, houses for the executioner and his assistants. At the four corners, the Chamber of Deputies, the Chamber of Peers, the Institute and the Royal Palace. Outside, there are the various services that supply the central enclosure, commerce, with its swindlers and its bankruptcies; industry and its furious struggles; the press, with its sophisms; the gambling dens; prostitution, the people dying of hunger or wallowing in debauchery, always ready to lend an ear to the voice of the Genius of Revolutions; the heartless rich... Lastly the ruthless war of all against all.

Foucault argues that the passage suggests we are a great distance from the *ancien régime*'s country of tortures and from the reformers' vision of justice meted out in public punishment on stocks:

The extract from *La Phalange* reminds us of some of the more important [principles]: that at the centre of this city, and as if to hold it in place, there is, not the 'centre of power', not a network of forces, but a multiple network of diverse elements – walls, space, institution, rules, discourse; that the model of the carceral city is not, therefore, the body of the king, with the powers that emanate from it, nor the contractual meeting of wills from which a body that was both individual and collective was born, but a strategic distribution of elements of different natures and levels.

The disciplinary society is somewhat ad hoc. Systems of normalization don't emanate from a central power, but from a network of overlapping and sometimes competing forces. The panopticon metaphor isn't a metaphor for society as a whole but instead a particular mechanism that has been particularly successful, reproducible and adaptable. In this reading, the Ring of Steel shares some characteristics with Foucault's disciplinary regime (strategic rearrangement of space, surveillance with the goal of changing behaviour) and some with the *ancien régime* (theatrical demonstrations of the power of the state). It isn't a carefully considered and constituted arrangement, but a series of accreted practices, accumulated in response to – and in anticipation of – various real and imagined threats.

This is at once painfully obvious – of course security regimes were changed in response to successful terrorist actions and in anticipation of more to come – and powerfully weird. Certainly, it's not what a traditional conception of liberal democracy teaches about the organization of Western society. Western societies are meant to be Nations of Laws, created by a Deliberative Body derived from a Constitution made up of various principles like equality, liberty and freedom of speech. But that's not what happens on the ground. Here's Foucault again: 'ultimately what presides over all these mechanisms is not the unitary functioning of an apparatus or an institution, but the necessity of combat and the rules of strategy.'

The story of the City and the Ring of Steel certainly has the flavour of combat. We see a series of moves and counter-moves between adversaries. The IRA tries to kill the prime minister; the government installs gates; the IRA launches mortars. The IRA wreaks havoc with a truck bomb; the City reconfigures itself to better control and prevent future attacks. This is literally combat, after all – the metaphor is clear.

But then, take a step back. Consider how odd it is that one of the achievements that the City police commissioner was most proud of was ecological. Fewer cars meant fewer bombs, sure, but also less pollution and an easier time for pedestrians. And in the wake of reduced security concerns, he hoped the measures would remain in place precisely because of these ancillary benefits. The reduction of air pollution by 15 percent in the City during the first year of the Ring's existence was used to justify its expansion later in the 1990s. How pleasant! Is Kelly's argument a bit of misdirection to keep these security measures alive in a hostile political atmosphere or a sincerely held Bentham-like belief in the myriad advantages of these systems? It hardly matters. Consciously or unconsciously, the disciplinary apparatus seeks to extend itself.

Secured Landscape

In the heightened paranoia of the post-9/11 environment, phys-ical barriers – similar to those used in the City to prevent traffic access or to distance cars from buildings – were installed around various potential targets. The old U.S. embassy at Grosvenor Square was seen as particularly vulnerable, and was subsequently surrounded by fences, Jersey barriers and armed guards. One side of the square was completely closed off to vehicular traffic. This is an example of post-hoc alter-ations to an already-built environment. Current security requirements demand a thirty-metre defensive perimeter, and there is no way a building like the current embassy – which is set in a posh London neighbourhood – can accommodate that stipulation. The real cutting edge of defensible architecture must be incorporated into the initial design stages of new construction.

To bake the latest techniques right into the walls is, after all, the panoptic dream. Bentham believed that with the right architecture, many of the worst and most brutalizing aspects of security would become unnecessary, as inmates would simply be rendered unable to harm others or themselves. This in turn would obviate the need to incur the costs (both psychological and financial) associated with such things, he writes.

> Upon all plans hitherto pursued, the thickest walls have been found occasionally unavailing: upon this plan, the thinnest would be sufficient – a circumstance which must operate, in a striking degree, towards a diminution of the expense.
>
> In this, as in every other application of the plan, you will find its lenient, not less conspicuous than its coercive, tendency; insomuch that, if you were to be asked who had most cause to wish for its adoption, you might find yourself at some loss to determine between the malefactors themselves, and those for whose sake they are consigned to punishment.

Foucault seems to believe more or less the same thing. In the layouts of schools, factories and prisons he can read the workings of disciplinary power.

> This infinitely scrupulous concern with surveillance is expressed in the architecture by innumerable petty mechanisms. These mechanisms can only be seen as unimportant if one forgets the role of this instrumentation, minor but flawless, in the progressive objectification

and the ever more subtle partitioning of individual behavior. The disciplinary institutions secreted a machinery of control that functioned like a microscope of conduct; the fine, analytical divisions that they created formed around men an apparatus of observation, recording, and training. How was one to subdivide the gaze in these observation machines? How was one to establish a network of communications between them? How was one so to arrange things that a homogeneous, continuous power would result from their calculated multiplicity?

The design of the new U.S. embassy in London – whose creation process began in 2008 with an estimated 2017 move-in date – offers a striking example. This time, instead of clumsily adding security features in response to threats, they will be incorporated from day one.

Security considerations began with the location. It is far outside the Square Mile, in Wandsworth on the south bank of the Thames, a site chosen explicitly for defensibility. Rather than being in a dense, crowded neighbourhood, the new embassy will be located in a relatively open light-industrial zone. Embassy security forces will have more control over the whole area, since their neighbours will be farther away.

In 2010, the Philadelphia architecture firm KieranTimberlake won the design competition for the facility itself. The U.S. government's official announcement enumerated the new building's virtues, a 'modern, welcoming, timeless, safe and energy efficient embassy for the 21st century.' Interestingly, the architecture firm's blog post about the design is flippant about security concerns, putting 'safety' in scare quotes when remarking on the design's lack of security walls. '[I]t's not a fortress,' architect James Timberlake said of the design. 'We are able to use the landscape as a security device. There's no wall and no fences.'

The security features for the new embassy will be miles more subtle than Grosvenor Square's reinforced-concrete planters. One side of the building is separated from the street with a rolling berm and multiple layers of gardens, which also serve as a barrier around the building to prevent cars from approaching the embassy. The other side is kept from the street by a semicircular lake (snidely called a 'moat' in the press, and for good reason, as it serves a security purpose as well as an aesthetic one). From the north side, a public park will be available, but other outdoor plazas around the building will be inaccessible to passersby, who must make their way through the security station before being granted entry. Those security features will be invisible from the outside, since the landscaping allows 'required secure boundaries' to be 'incised into the hillside and out of view.'

All of this distance-creation has a name: *standoff*. Vehicle-carried bombs remain the primary security concern, and it's easier to protect a building by reinforcing the space around it than by reinforcing the building itself. Security experts determine the amount of space and/or stopping power required to prevent a vehicle from getting from the street to the building. Reinforced planters, trees and street furniture all contribute to standoff distance, as do, more troublingly, public plazas and sidewalk cafés.

Some of the theory behind this new type of architecture comes from the early 1970s, in a book called *Defensible Space*, by American architect and city planner Oscar Newman. In it, Newman sets up his plan for social control and crime prevention through the design of communities. His work builds on Jane Jacobs's *The Death and Life of Great American Cities*, in which she encourages 'eyes on the street' for safety and crime reduction. If streets are busy and full of people, she reasons, fewer crimes will be committed. Newman expanded that idea, suggesting that residents should feel territorial about the communal spaces outside their own homes. If their homes are physically oriented toward the street, and they feel responsible for those spaces, they will be more likely to keep an eye out for anything untoward.

By the 1980s and 1990s, Newman had further expanded his idea and folded it in with Crime Prevention Through Environmental Design, a 1970s initiative from the criminologist C. Ray Jeffery. CPTED incorporates more alteration of the built environment than Newman's original study, and also works for commercial or office districts rather than strictly residential zones. The notion is a very Benthamite one: that the behaviour of residents and visitors can be changed by the careful design of space.

According to Newman and Jeffery, if you want to build a safe space, there are a few principles to follow. First, you want to make sure casual surveillance is easy. Have lots of windows, keep the fences and bushes nice and low, and avoid bright lights – and the deep shadows that accompany them – for nighttime visibility. You also want to control entry to your building with locks and sensors (in the business, this is called 'target hardening'). But, most importantly for the types of vulnerable buildings we're talking about, you want to control the physical shape of the site itself. That means using whatever means available to control access to the building – that's where the landscaping and moats come in – forming boundaries between the street and the building. All of this is intended to reduce the incidence of crime, or at least enable the building occupants to spot suspicious activity and head it off at the pass.

This is all about a movement toward permanent solutions rather than temporary, ad hoc ones. Architects would rather not see their work marred by fencing and concrete blocks, and the users of the space would rather not feel like they live or work in a war zone. And as security becomes more discreet, safeguards are becoming indistinguishable from decorative embellishments.

To use another example in London, Emirates Stadium in Holloway is a sixty-thousand-seat football ground. Between the road and one entrance sit huge concrete letters spelling out the name of the stadium's home football club, Arsenal. While the letters are a popular photo-op location for club supporters, their main function is to prevent cars from accessing the stadium over the south bridge. In those letters, we can hear the distant roar of battle.

As they conceptualized the Ring of Steel, London's city planners called it 'fortress urbanism.' Thinking of castles, we realized that the U.K. has been awash in security landscapes for centuries. Crenellated battlements served an aesthetic purpose as well as a practical one, and they certainly signified high status, since the builder had to obtain a licence to crenellate before doing so. Even disguised landscape security features are not new; the English landed gentry have been preserving their views (and protecting their livestock) with sunken walls called ha-has since before the Norman conquest. Weapons and tactics change, security measures change and then the next generation of buildings and street furniture incorporate those changes. Today, crenellations serve only a decorative function.

In large part, the means of disguising security features used by buildings like the new American embassy are designed to reduce the climate of fear that might otherwise accompany a highly securitized environment. The public realm should be as pretty as it ever was, but underneath the velvet glove of its aesthetically pleasing and useful features lies a true, iron-fisted security purpose. Security features become ubiquitous where they were once exceptional. They are being designed to blend into the landscape. Of course, some security measures are not written on the spaces themselves, but instead watch over them from above.

Wired Audience

This book isn't about cameras, no matter how ubiquitous, charismatic and emblematic of the entire hidden surveillance infrastructure they may be. There's a lot more to surveillance networks than cameras. But this section is the exception. Here, we're talking about cameras – large numbers of them.

Bentham would have loved closed-circuit television and contemporary security cameras. He spends a considerable portion of *Panopticon* working out the physical problem of setting up a situation where the guards operating in the tower can see without being seen. In his postscript, he confesses to some flaws in his initial design:

> Upon the first crude conception, as stated in the Letters, my hope had been, that by the help of blinds and screens, the faculty of invisible inspection might have been enjoyed in perfection by the whole number of persons occupying the central part, wherever they were placed in it, and whether in motion or at rest. I am now assured, and I fear with truth, that these expectations were in some respects too sanguine. I mean, as to what concerns ideal and absolute perfection: at the same time that for real service, their completion, I trust, will not be found to have sustained any material abatement.
>
> Were I to persist in endeavouring to give this property of invisibility with regard to the cells, as well to the person of the inspector as to every part of the large circle in which I place him, and to every object in it, his situation would stand exposed, I am assured, to this dilemma: if he has light enough to do any business, he will be seen, whatever I can do, from the cells: if there is not light enough there for him to be seen from the cells, there will not be light enough to enable him to do his business.

CCTV solves Bentham's problem. Thanks to a marvel of electronics, the physical need for reciprocity in illumination is broken. The camera can be seen but not its operator, if operator there be. On the high end, the camera can be equipped with inhuman sight via infrared and low-light vision. It can be networked and combined into a bank of monitors allowing the operator the inhuman ability to zip around in space. It can be linked to recording media, allowing the operator the inhuman ability to remember everything and zip around in time. On the low end, if funds are tight, you don't even need the camera at all. In many situations, an empty CCTV chassis will do.

After the City bombings in the early 1990s, one of the innovations brought in by the City police force was the CameraWatch program. This was a public-private partnership, where the police logged all CCTV systems on private businesses in the area, and encouraged them to share information where possible.

The Ring of Steel combines physical structures with these cameras. Some are standard CCTV, but others are ANPR cameras, which feature automatic number plate recognition. The evolution of the ANPR network is instructive. The cameras were first introduced in the 1980s, in an attempt to reduce auto theft. They became commonplace in the U.K. over the course of the 1990s. Today, the stated purpose for London's ANPR cameras is to administer traffic congestion charges. Building on the much-touted environmental successes of the City's Ring of Steel, the network automatically bills drivers who enter a twelve-square-kilometre congestion zone, extending the pollution-reduction benefits to more of the city. Over and over, the network is repurposed as it steadily expands. In 2001, British licence-plate design was changed to make plates easier for the cameras to read.

Some CCTV cameras run by local governments in the U.K. are even equipped to talk back. They have loudspeakers installed, so the operator can speak to a potential offender at a safe distance. Given that Bentham spends several pages working through the design of speaking tubes to allow the watchers in the tower to communicate with inmates, you can bet he'd install these without delay

This has us thinking about the weird theatricality of surveillance and safety. The key to the Panopticon is that you are aware that you are potentially being watched. The people must be aware that these structures exist. The camera is the perfect solution to the issue of one-sidedness. A camera suggests you can be seen, whether it is a dummy or a real one.

Samuel and Jeremy Bentham's original Panopticon project had a lot to do with theatricality as well. Samuel was working for Potemkin, whose namesake villages were famously (and apocryphally) one-dimensional, meant only to look good for the Empress Catherine's trip through White Russia. The panopticon design Samuel proposed was part of that theatrical presentation as well – it was to demonstrate the newly mobilized industrial might of the Russian peasantry.

His brother was possibly more preoccupied with the theatre. In the postscript to *Panopticon*, Jeremy Bentham suggested that one of the administrators of the panoptic prison ought to be a theatre manager:

> *Nihil ex scenâ*, says Lord Bacon, speaking of procedure in the civil branch of the law: *Multum ex scenâ*, I will venture to say, speaking of the penal. The disagreement is but verbal: *Scena*, in the language of the noble philosopher, means *lying*: in mine, *scena* is but *scenery*. To say, *Multum ex scenâ*, is to say, lose no occasion of speaking to the eye. In a well-composed committee of penal law, I know not a more essential personage than the manager of a theatre.

The Panopticon is to serve a public purpose as well as a correctional one. It is the theatre manager who knows how to put on the 'show' of punishment (here, Bentham's plan works at cross-purposes to Foucault's argument, which suggests that in a disciplinary society, spectacles of punishment are replaced with the knowledge that you'll be caught). In Bentham, it is by seeing the punishment occur that it retains its power. Our modern CCTV cameras place that theatrical watcher at a degree of remove, but she is still assumed to be there. Bill Brown, an artist with the pro-privacy Surveillance Camera Players, an activist theatre group who perform specifically adapted plays directly in front of surveillance cameras, said in an interview in 2003: 'Here, "theatre" is a very interesting word because the surveillance cameras are attempting to stage a theater of conformity, so that even before artists or Situationists arrived to see the dramatic potential, they're already turning the streets into stages and people perform either by ignoring the cameras, or they know that they're there and perform in conformity with societal norms.'

There are elements of the theatrical in other arenas of security. Bruce Schneier, a security and privacy specialist and cryptographer, calls the rituals of security performed every day at airports and other locations 'security theatre.' Checkpoints, scanners, sensors and CCTV networks have proliferated. Procedures for travellers tend to be knee-jerk reactions to specific threats, and are rescinded or changed seemingly on a whim. Schneier believes that while some procedures adopted since September 2001 have had a measurable effect on safety (such as reinforcing cockpit doors on planes and making sure travellers always fly with their luggage), the rest are there only to make the public feel as if something is being done. Rather than being purely disciplinary, entirely a product of Foucault's panoptic world, security theatre has an element of the *ancien régime*, with its insistence on the performance of power in front of the public.

Foucault mentions the carceral city only briefly in *Discipline & Punish*, near its conclusion. His friend Gilles Deleuze, the

French philosopher, wrote about his colleague's work in 1992, eight years after Foucault's death. He thought that Foucault had adeptly described the difference between the sovereign society of the early modern period and the disciplinary society of the eighteenth and nineteenth centuries. But he hadn't described the next stage, which Deleuze called the 'societies of control.'

This new society was one where the mechanisms of control filter out from the institutions Foucault described, into the wider social world. Instead of prison sentences, you have house arrest enforced by a GPS-enabled ankle monitor. Instead of the factory floor, you have the diverse, diffuse corporation, monitoring you as both a customer and an employee. Deleuze describes a world of barriers, automatically opening or closing according to one's ID card, but 'what counts is not the barrier but the computer that tracks each person's position.' While the physical barriers around the City of London protect only that oh-so-economically vital square mile, the electronic techniques that form the other layer of the Ring of Steel have become commonplace around the U.K. and in other world cities. The fortress has become a virtual one.

The original justification for the Ring of Steel had become essentially obsolete in the mid-1990s, but the Ring itself did not disappear. In fact, in 1997, it was expanded westward to include sites like St. Paul's Cathedral, and cameras were improved with zoom capabilities, 360-degree swivelling and lights, technologies developed in the first Gulf War. The last couple of years of the 1990s were marked by serious anti-capitalist demonstrations around the world, including London. While the Ring of Steel couldn't stop pedestrian protesters from entering the City, the cameras could certainly record their identities for later prosecution. The perceived level of risk in London has shifted many times over the last few decades, but for the last twenty years, the basic architecture of the Ring has only ever grown.

Please Empty Your Pockets and Place the Contents in the Tray

The U.S. Transportation Security Administration was created on November 19, 2001, in the mad rush to securitization that followed the September 11 attacks. Before that date, airport security had been up to the airlines themselves, and private companies contracted by individual airports.

Because the speed of architecture does not often match the speed of policy, many airports are perfect examples of new security regimes being mapped over spaces designed for older regimes. Any airport built before the mid-1970s basically had no spatial provisions for security. In the late 1960s, armed hijackers began to take control of commercial planes. From 1968 to 1972, a period known as the golden age of hijacking, over 130 American planes were diverted, usually to Cuba.

Remarkably, it took years for anything to be done about this. At the time, there were no metal detectors or screenings at airports, and non-ticket-holders could climb the stairs and board a flight unassailed. The airline industry – and its powerful lobby – was terrified that any security measures would result in a populace unwilling to fly. All of this foot-dragging meant that metal detectors weren't mandatory until 1973.

Suddenly, lots of space had to be created in airports where no such spaces had existed before. The problem only got worse after 2001. Lengthy security cordons, private rooms for pat-downs, metal detectors, baggage screeners and full-body scanners all require room. Older airports had to be retrofitted, sometimes awkwardly, but new buildings are able to design security features in from the beginning. Architectural solutions to potential violence are still routinely proposed. For instance, faster-moving lineups not only mean happier travellers, but that fewer potential casualties will be in that generally crowded area in case of a luggage bomb.

'*Your occasional vigilance will not do*, says an objector: *Your prisoner will make experiments upon it, discover when Argus nods, and make his advantage of the discovery. He will hazard a venial transgression at a venture: that unnoticed, he will go on to more material ones.* Will he? I will soon put an end to his experiments: or rather, to be beforehand with him, I will take care he shall not think of making any. I will single out one of the most untoward of the prisoners. I will keep an unintermitted watch upon him. I will watch until I observe a transgression. I will minute it down. I will wait for another: I will note that down too. I will lie by for a whole day: he shall do as he pleases that day, so long as he does not venture at something too serious to be endured. The next day I produce the list to him. – *You thought yourself undiscovered: you abused my indulgence: see how you were mistaken. Another time, you may have rope for two days, ten days: the longer it is, the heavier it will fall upon you. Learn from this, all of you, that in this house transgression never can be safe.* Will the policy be cruel? – No; it will be kind: it will prevent transgressing; it will save punishing.'

– Jeremy Bentham, *Panopticon; or,*
The Inspection-House

'And, although the universal juridicism of modern society seems to fix limits on the exercise of power, its universally widespread panopticism enables it to operate, on the underside of the law, a machinery that is both immense and minute, which supports, reinforces, multiplies the asymmetry of power and undermines the limits that are traced around the law.'

– Michel Foucault, *Discipline & Punish*

Things are different in Oakland, California. Where London's Ring of Steel is essentially a postmodern riff on the city's original fortifications from about 200 CE, the surveillance infrastructure in Oakland is more like a local manifestation of the ubiquitous surveillance by networked state entities such as the National Security Agency. Where London's perimeter essentially traces the stone walls built by the Romans — enhanced and improved with twentieth- and twenty-first-century technology — the network of surveillance in Oakland is almost impossible to conceptualize in a purely physical metaphor.

These tendrils of surveillance have been collected under the rubric of the Domain Awareness Center. The first phase of the surveillance hub was proposed back in 2008. The DAC was meant to aggregate the information from CCTV cameras, licence-plate readers, thermal imaging cameras, motion detectors, traffic cameras and sound recorders in order to prevent crime in the city. The centre itself would be the collection point for all of this data, coordinating official responses to terrorism, natural disasters and ordinary crime.

Oakland sits on the east side of San Francisco Bay. It consists of about 145 square kilometres of land with another fifty-seven square kilometres of water. Two-thirds of the city rests on the flat plain of the East Bay, with the other third rising into the foothills and hills of the East Bay range. A good portion of the shore is given over to container piers.

Oakland is considered one of the most dangerous cities in the U.S. Both violent and property crimes have been well above the national average since the turn of the twenty-first century, and the rates weren't great before that, either. The rise in crime, which began back in the 1960s, has been attributed to both a loss of significant manufacturing jobs and changes in police tactics where youth gangs are concerned. During that decade, gang members began to age out of their teenage years and violence increased. Rather than expanding resources, the approach to gangs changed from social work–oriented (persuading kids to join youth centres or return to school) to more enforcement-based methods.

Oakland's police department is chronically understaffed. In 2011, the city averaged three shootings a day. In 2012, there was one robbery for every ninety-one residents. With only 654 officers as of April 2014, Oakland's police force has around sixteen officers per 10,000 people, compared to forty-four per 10,000 in N.Y.C. and twenty-nine per 10,000 in San Francisco. The city's complement of police is consistently under the average for the rest of the state of California as well. Lobbyist group Oakland Residents for Peaceful Neighbourhoods calls it 'the City with Half a Police Department.'

Bentham would be delighted to offer a solution to this scenario. His Panopticon was intended as a labour-saving device, after all. With its network of connected cameras and sensors, the DAC seems to surpass Bentham's designs, neatly solving the problem he struggled most with – how to see without being seen. The DAC would allow a few officers to monitor many parts of the city at once. Even if an officer isn't watching, the camera presumably is, and those cameras are supposed to deter criminals by their very presence.

Does CCTV actually prevent crime? The question is hardly settled. Current doctrine is that CCTV is supposed to perform a deterrent function, as well as helping with investigations after a crime has been committed. The usefulness of the camera in investigations is relatively easy to measure. If cameras are used to find suspects and secure conviction, they are useful. But the causal link between a camera installation and a drop in crime is much harder to prove. If crime drops, it's almost impossible to say whether it's the camera, since cameras are rarely the sole intervention. Installation of cameras might coincide with more police patrols, for instance, or it may be that the problem spots were temporary outliers and the drop is simply reversion to the mean. Many camera systems go unwatched. Washington, D.C., installed seventy-three cameras beginning in 2006 and didn't start monitoring the live feeds until two years later.

CCTV is hardly the unalloyed good that it is sometimes assumed to be, and it is very probably only useful in preventing certain types of crime in certain types of spaces. Deterrence works only when the potential criminal is thinking clearly, in contrast to Bentham's image of the rationally self-interested individual. This means that relatively well-thought-out property crime is more likely to be prevented by cameras than violent crime, which might involve an intoxicated perpetrator. Major studies done in the mid-2000s by the Department of Justice in the U.S. and the Home Office in the U.K. did not come to clear conclusions. The DOJ suggested small systems within defined areas might be most useful, and the Home Office noted that prevention objectives need to be specific and planned ahead of time. With this in mind, let's head back to Oakland.

A report by the Oakland police from July 2008, written in support of the DAC scheme, seems to have swallowed – hook, line and sinker – the idea that surveillance reduces crime. However, rather than providing any data to prove that presumption, the report offers a mere *two* anecdotal examples of crimes foiled by surveillance cameras from other American police departments. The memo outlines the basics of what would become the DAC project: a network of public and private cameras (similar to London's CameraWatch) in which some are static, some are redeployable (i.e., transferrable to 'hot spots' as needed) and some are mounted to vehicles; there are also licence-plate readers and mics that listen for gunfire – all monitored from a single 'fusion centre.' In addition to the existing surveillance devices, the report proposes cameras in schools, public housing projects, the BART transit system and public libraries.

The tone of the memo is almost adorable in its hopefulness. The surveillance hub will be a panacea for the city, apparently. A section of the report lists corollary benefits to the surveillance regime as including:

- *Economic*: With the reduction of crime, the City may experience economic growth through business development, which will bring consumers who may contribute to the economy.
- *Environmental*: Crime breeds blight and degradation of a community; Surveillance cameras will help reduce crime, thereby creating a cleaner City, motivating citizens to get involved in the Department's efforts to improve the quality of life in the City of Oakland.
- *Social Equity*: By installing surveillance cameras throughout the City of Oakland, the Department will have an opportunity to enhance its investigative efforts, and provide a deterrent to criminal activity, effectively reducing crime in Oakland. Reduced crime will enhance the quality of life in Oakland.

So, according to the Oakland police, surveillance means better investigation, which means less crime, which means better quality of life. And somehow this will generate social equity? Less crime means less…garbage? Even the wide-eyed optimism of the report is tempered when it comes to clarifying economic benefits, which are cautiously stated, bookended with non-committal 'may's. The whole section would look familiar to anyone who's ever fudged a job application: shoehorn your actual skills and objectives into their required categories, and sort out the details later.

Let's talk for a minute about some of the technology used in the DAC. As mentioned, the network was intended to bring together information from CCTV cameras, licence-plate trackers and ShotSpotter mics to give a full picture of what is going on in the city. We've already heard about the former two surveillance technologies, but let's touch upon the last, as it's an unusual audio-only technology. ShotSpotters are special microphones or sensors, set up around an area under observation and networked into a processing unit. They are used to echolocate gunshots and triangulate where they come from. This can be complicated in a downtown location, where sound is deflected off buildings. The idea is that using the ShotSpotters, officers can be dispatched to the scene immediately, rather than waiting for a bystander to call 911. On top of that, there are exciting public education opportunities. Oakland publishes reports on its website, complete with maps of the neighbourhoods where gunshots were detected. A prospective homebuyer can check her new neighbourhood for incidences of shots fired on a month-to-month basis.

The DAC proposal is full of whiz-bang technology like this. The tech fulfills two functions: first, it reduces the number of officers who need to be on the street, and second, it gives an impression of the exciting and new, which attracts funding and partners.

Bentham's Panopticon letters are similarly enthusiastic about technical solutions to social problems. He spends considerable time on the lighting, the innovative new sewage and plumbing systems, and an intricate mechanism of gears and speaking tubes for communicating with the prisoners.

The problem with whiz-bang new tech is that it often has bugs. A 2012 article in the *Yale Daily News* tells how a ShotSpotter installation in New Haven, Connecticut, had a tendency to report false positives where no gunfire had happened and yet failed to hear the city's first shooting-related homicide of the year. A software update was reported to be on the way.

In March 2014, *SFGate* reported that the Oakland Police Department was considering dropping ShotSpotter. The system costs $264,000 a year and police contend that the information it gave them was redundant – after an alert, residents were calling in the crimes just fine on their own. The article quotes from several residents who felt otherwise:

> East Oakland residents and their City Council representatives say they don't want police to eliminate ShotSpotter. Knowing that sensors are monitoring – and documenting – gunfire is comforting, residents said, especially when they feel otherwise ignored and forgotten by downtown city leaders.
>
> 'I think they spend a lot of money on (stuff) that isn't necessary, but this seems necessary,' said Jaton Hurt, 22, who lives on 83rd Avenue in an area where ShotSpotter counted 21 incidents of gunfire in February. 'I would rather them know where gunshots are.'
>
> Hurt, who works as a security guard, said he wondered if police wanted to get rid of ShotSpotter so they didn't have to respond to every gunshot call.

Building Domain Awareness

In the 2008 report proposing the DAC, the authors open by noting the tens of millions of dollars needed to build the project and the million or two needed annually to keep it running. 'Currently,' it says, 'the Department has not identified funding for this project; however, staff is actively seeking possible grant opportunities that may be available to help fund this project.'

In September 2009, they found some of that money in a $2.9 million FEMA grant to the Port of Oakland. The 2008 report barely mentions the port, noting briefly that its cameras would be included in the DAC. 'The ability to view Port-owned cameras will provide valuable information when responding to, or investigating critical incidents. For example, in the event of a hazardous chemical spill staff will be able to respond and view the scene prior to arrival. This could provide critical information related to the perimeter of the scene and the need for any specialized equipment.' The law enforcement aspect is almost an afterthought, meriting about half a sentence: 'The Port cameras monitor both intersections and freeway traffic, which would allow for locating wanted vehicles or evaluating traffic conditions during a response to emergencies.'

So why start with the afterthought? Terrorism. Specifically, the availability of federal money to combat it. The mechanisms of discipline are fluid indeed, happy to rewrite their pitches according to the dominant concern of the day, be it efficiency, crime, terror, safety, health or the environment.

A Home Office report in 2005 predicted Oakland's enthusiasm for technological solutions to crime and terrorism problems. The report was prepared as an evaluation of thirteen new CCTV networks around the U.K. They found very mixed results in terms of effectiveness in crime reduction. The authors noted that some successes with CCTV in the 1990s led to 'a universal assumption that CCTV was a "good thing,"' which was backed up by the Home Office's own endorsement of camera systems. The Home Office made millions of pounds of funding for CCTV available to local authorities, starting in 1998. The report noted that some cities and towns had subsequently requested money for CCTV systems, whether or not there was an identified need for those systems. In some situations, other less costly measures − like gates or lighting improvements − might have been more effective, but were not conveniently grant-supported. But when money *is* made available, it is difficult for cash-strapped cities not to jump at the opportunity to appear *tough on crime* to their citizens. Similarly, when Homeland Security made funds available for counter-terrorism initiatives, it was impossible for Oakland to resist.

The Port of Oakland was the first U.S. port on the west coast built to accept container ships, and in 1959 became the first port to run land-based cranes custom-made for containers, designed and built for the Hawaii-based Matson Navigation Company. The Port of Oakland now handles more cargo containers than all but four U.S. ports (including New York/New Jersey) and is the fifteenth largest by tons. The first port in the area was across the bay in San Francisco, but much as New Jersey supplanted Manhattan, Oakland's superior access to land transportation made it a better location for containers. When container ships first came in, the San Francisco port director refused to build special piers for them, believing container shipping to be a fad. So all container shipping went to Oakland, which was willing to accommodate it.

The port area also features an airport, first established in 1927. When jets became common in the early 1960s, the airport required longer runways. The shallows of the San Francisco Bay was the chosen spot. Dredge boats spat up sand, and the shallows were drained and diked. In a 1962 promotional video about the construction, the narrator exults that the airport was designed to 'meet the requirements of jet-age commerce.' Oakland was moving into a new commercial era.

Because ports are liminal spaces, where goods and people enter and leave the country, they are prone to crime of various kinds, including smuggling, human trafficking and terrorism, that (currently) greatest bugbear of them all. Like any port zone, Oakland's has a close relationship with criminal and otherwise-sketchy activities. In Oakland, that relationship is built right into the city's founding. In 1850, a Columbia College law graduate named Horace Carpentier arrived in what was then the village of Contra Costa. In the next few years, he would see the town incorporated as Oakland, become its mayor and orchestrate a land grab in which he took control of the entire waterfront in exchange for building a schoolhouse, some wharves and a cash payment of five dollars. This set off decades of dispute about the ownership of the waterfront land. It wasn't until 1907 that the city finally ousted Carpentier completely and took control over the port area itself.

Unlike the port of New York/New Jersey, elements of which are infamously mob-run, the Port of Oakland seems relatively quiet on the organized-crime front. The Attorney General's 2007 report to the California Legislature suggests that organized-crime groups and gangs do participate in cargo theft, but cargo theft didn't even merit a mention in the 2009 and 2010 editions. The only smuggling noted at all happens on the Mexican border. Instead of organized crime, the port officials here worry about the labour movement. Port of Oakland labour is organized by the International Longshore and Warehouse Union, which controls all twenty-nine of the U.S. ports on the Pacific, including Alaska and Hawaii.

Labour-related port shutdowns can have a huge economic impact. In September 2002, the ILWU on the west coast of the U.S. staged a work slowdown during their contract negotiations. The Pacific Maritime Association responded with a lockout, which shut down the twenty-nine Pacific ports entirely. After eleven days, President George W. Bush intervened, invoking the Taft-Hartley or Labor-Management Relations Act to send 10,500 longshoremen back to work and reopen the docks. The 1947 act allows presidents to seek injunctions against strikes that 'imperil the national health or safety.' Bush's main concern at the time was military supply chains, which often make use of civilian container ships. The president's military actions in the Middle East at the time required working Pacific coast ports, so he ordered union members back to work. The ILWU responded on May Day 2008 by walking off the job in protest of the still-ongoing Iraq War. In 2002, the cost of the port shutdown had been estimated at about $2 billion a day. (That approximation is questionable, since it assumes all cargo that would have been handled at those ports was lost, rather than being diverted to other ports of entry.) Similar estimates show up in documents like *Port and Maritime Security: Background and Issues for Congress*, which looked at the potential impact of a terrorist strike in terms of the economic effects of a labour strike (it pegged the damage at $1 billion a day for the first five days, then rising sharply).

Ports are considered an important vector for large-scale terrorist acts. Even before 2001, ports and shipping were identified as potential terrorist targets. The general attitude was more or less 'This isn't safe, but it's probably fine.' While recognizing that security was not terribly stringent and that ports were vulnerable if an attack were to actually occur, the FBI considered the likelihood of an attack on an American port to be low. In 1999, the FBI's *30 Years of Terrorism* report didn't see fit to mention port security. Even in 2006, time spent investigating maritime terrorism was filed under 'Counterterrorism Preparedness: Other.'

Ships themselves are at greater risk in port zones than when they are in the deep sea. When approaching or in port zones, they are moving slowly (if at all). The USS *Cole*, for example, was bombed in 2000 while in port in Yemen. Container ships, which are generally unarmed and have small crews, have it worse. Any time the container is not moving, it is vulnerable both to thieves and to terrorists. 'Goods at rest are goods at risk' is how the Public Policy Institute of California puts it in a report on port protection.

The fact that the port is surrounded by a city is seen as dangerous, too. In a 2005 report for the U.S. Congress on port security, the authors suggests that cities built around ports provide hiding spots for terrorists while they wait to attack the port itself. Worse yet, if an urban port were attacked, the consequences would be correspondingly more devastating because of the higher nearby population.

There are two versions of the story of the link between the port and the city and the DAC. In one version, the surveillance of the city comes first, with the DAC being a kind of afterthought that takes advantage of FEMA's concentration on terror to repurpose the program and include the port. In the other version, security for the port came first, and sometime in 2009–2010, the DAC plan was expanded to include the whole city. As of 2014, thanks to sustained public protest, Oakland city council has rolled back the project, and it is again primarily about protecting the port.

But what if the DAC was never intended to reduce crime, or even to prevent terrorism? There is a pervasive view in the activist community in Oakland that the DAC was always intended to watch over *them*.

Activist Oakland

This chapter was meant to be about Occupy Oakland.

The first OO encampment was established on October 10, 2011, less than a month after the launch of Occupy Wall Street. The protesters set up at Frank H. Ogawa Plaza in the shadow of Oakland's city hall, and expanded to Snow Park a week later. The camps were cleared out on October 25, re-established on October 26 and cleared again on November 14.

We want to talk about Occupy Oakland because, by the end of *Discipline & Punish*, Foucault has painted a pretty comprehensive picture of carceral cities in a carceral society. And while the patterns he points to seem to have evolved and intensified today, there are also sites of resistance and transformation. Or sites that simply don't easily fit into the disciplinary mould.

Occupy Wall Street started out focused on the excesses of the financial industry, and the consequent financial crash that threw an already-precarious economy into total disarray with few consequences for those responsible and plenty of consequences for those caught up in the turbulence. Occupy Oakland grew out of that, but from the start also had much to say about the abuses of the local police. When they set up camp in Frank H. Ogawa Plaza, they renamed the space for Oscar Grant, who had been killed by transit police a couple of years prior.

Bentham's Panopticon is a highly hierarchical affair, with prisoners at the periphery and jailers at the centre, themselves subjected to external inspection from magistrates and other 'Men of Quality.' This is the pattern Foucault takes as emblematic of contemporary society – the relationship between Oakland's residents, its police force and the political body is far more complex.

When Occupy Oakland and allies called for a general strike on November 2, 2011, Mayor Jean Quan issued a memo that gave all civil servants the day off – except for the police. 'That's hundreds of City workers encouraged to take off work to participate in the protest against "the establishment,"' wrote the Oakland Police Officers' Association in an open letter. 'But aren't the Mayor and her Administration part of the establishment they are paying City employees to protest? Is it the City's intention to have City employees on both sides of a skirmish line? It is all very confusing to us.'

According to a 2013 investigation by the *East Bay Express*, emails sent during 2012–2013 between city officials, police and contractors revealed no mentions of robberies, homicides or other crimes that might be caught by the nascent DAC. Instead, they refer to monitoring political protesters:

> This aspect of the DAC first became public in August when Renee Domingo, director of Oakland's Emergency Management Services Division and the head of the DAC project team, published an article in the government

trade publication *Public CEO* justifying the need for the surveillance hub. 'Oakland's long history of civil discourse and protest adds to the need [for the Domain Awareness Center],' Domingo wrote. 'The Oakland Emergency Operations Center has been partially or fully activated more than 30 times in the past three years to respond to large demonstrations and protests.

Domingo isn't wrong about Oakland's long history of civil discourse. The Black Panther Party for Self-Defense was formed in Oakland in 1966, a response to the brutalization of black neighbourhoods by the police. A Stop the Draft Week protest began at the Oakland Armed Forces Induction Center on Clay Street in October 1967 – thousands of people attempted to shut down the centre, and were met with riot police. Clubs and tear gas were used to clear the streets, to general public outcry.

Concordia University professor Brady Thomas Heiner argues that Foucault owes a great deal of the thinking that led to *Discipline & Punish* to an encounter with the Black Panthers. 'Foucault's shift from archaeological inquiry to genealogical critique is fundamentally motivated by his encounter with American-style racism and class struggle,' writes Heiner, 'and by his engagement with the political philosophies and documented struggles of the BPP.' Heiner's thesis remains controversial, necessarily relying on circumstantial evidence to make the case that an exposure to Black Panther thinking changed the course of Foucault's work and was buried. Some relationship exists. It is clear that Foucault was co-author of *L'Assassinat de George Jackson*, a pamphlet released by the Groupe d'information sur les prisons, an organization that agitated for the dissemination of information about the state of French prisons. The pamphlet says the death of George Jackson during an alleged escape attempt was a political assassination by U.S. authorities. Foucault's involvement with the GIP preceded (and certainly heavily influenced) the writing of *Discipline & Punish*.

It'd be hard to argue that things in Oakland have gotten much better since the 1960s. Starting in 2003, the Oakland Police Department has been under federal oversight as part of a settlement with the 119 people who pressed civil rights lawsuits for unlawful beatings and detention as part of a police corruption scandal. In 2012, the department was threatened with being placed under federal receivership when the district court ruled that it had failed to live up to the settlement's terms.

In addition to general concerns about racism and corruption, the OPD has a contentious history with anti-war and anti-capitalist protesters. In 2003, two Oakland police officers infiltrated an anti–Iraq War protest. The officers managed to be elected to influential positions within the organization and determined the route of the protest. They had become interested in the protest at an earlier march, which had shut down the Port of Oakland and resulted in injuries to protesters and longshoremen from police rubber bullets. The California Anti-Terrorism Information Center (a post-September 11 state database on terrorist activities) had posted an alert about the upcoming action in April. This was not the first equation of protest activities to terrorism. The California organized-crime reports of both 2007/2008 and 2009/2010 refer to 'anarchist criminal extremists' and 'anti-tax sovereign citizen extremists' as sub-types of domestic terrorists.

Most protests these days are subject to some manner of negotiation with the police: police are informed that an action is going to happen, the planned route of marches, etc. Occupy Oakland, however, refused to negotiate with the cops and obtained no permits. Normally, negotiation between authorities and protesters is used to limit the disruption caused by the protest and mitigate violent reactions from police. This means that any actions that stray outside the agreed-upon parameters can be met with police violence with less risk of public disapproval. When a permit to erect a teepee was eventually sought by one committee of Occupy Oakland, the terms of that permit were used to crack down on other activities in the park, and, ultimately, to justify the raids and arrests in December 2011, as the police searched for evidence of protesters dwelling in the park, which was not allowed under the teepee permit terms.

Occupy Oakland was constantly monitored by police, but the surveillance was not one-way. Occupiers also watched, filmed and photographed the cops. The police, in response, used high-powered LED flashlights to blow out the cameras' light meters, and covered their badge numbers to make themselves invisible again. Many Occupy camps also had homegrown media, in the form of self-appointed livestreamers who broadcast from their laptops and cellphones. Some camps set up regular publications, as in the case of Occupy Portland, which ran an online magazine called the *Portland Occupier*. These outlets worked to make Occupy and the police surrounding it visible to the wider world.

Occupy camps can be seen as attempts to carve out a place for an alternative society within existing cities. They had to deal with the problems of a society, since that's what they were making on a small scale. In its efforts to forestall a crackdown and to take care of its participants, Occupy Oakland had to be a self-policing community. Arguably, this is exactly what Bentham would have wanted. The Panopticon was supposed to be automatic, a sort of machine that would operate without an operator.

There were high-profile incidences of police violence relating to Occupy Oakland. In one instance, an Oakland man named Scott Campbell was filming police officers during the general strike in November 2011, and an officer asked him to step back. He complied, but was hit with a rubber bullet anyway. Outrage followed when he released his video to the public. Most famously, Iraq War veteran and Occupy participant Scott Olsen was shot in the head with a beanbag by a SWAT team officer. All in all, the police department dealt with over one thousand complaints about police behaviour during Occupy. A dozen Occupy Oakland protesters sued the OPD, alleging excessive force suffered on October 25, 2011, when they were attempting to reoccupy the camp after a clearing-out. In July 2013, they were awarded nearly $1.2 million in damages by the U.S. District Court of Northern California.

Occupy Hygiene

Foucault writes:

> And, for [the transformation of individuals], the carceral apparatus has recourse to three great schemata: the politico-moral schema of individual isolation and hierarchy; the economic model of force applied to compulsory work; the technico-medical model of cure and normalization. The cell, the workshop, the hospital. The margin by which the prison exceeds detention is filled in fact by techniques of a disciplinary type. And this disciplinary addition to the juridical is what, in short, is called the 'penitentiary.'

The Occupy Oakland camp gives us an opportunity to look at a space where Foucault's carceral apparatus works across both the politico-moral schema and the technico-medical. Throughout this book, we've touched frequently on the workshop and the cell. But the hospital has remained relatively unexamined. The hospital must control its patients to prevent contamination and the dispersal of disease. The same techniques are employed outside the hospital, to control and direct the general population.

Quarantine has been used since the days of the Black Death to prevent people who might be sick from passing that illness along. New arrivals who aren't showing symptoms are isolated from the rest of the population, and are watched to see if they become sick before they are allowed entry. Narratives about illness and contamination often go hand-in-hand with xenophobic attitudes, with outsiders suspected of carrying infection that might spread through the homeland. Port cities particularly are subject to this logic. Before air travel, seaports were the most important vectors for contagious disease, providing entry not just to people and goods from other parts of the world, but also to illnesses.

Bentham had something to say about sanitation. In the postcript to *Panopticon* (which is, in fact, more voluminous by several times than the letters themselves, and the site of much of his detail-oriented fussing), he has a section on the health and cleanliness of the prisoner: '[Cleanliness] is an antidote against sloth: and keeps alive the idea of decent restraint, and the habit of circumspection. Moral purity and physical are spoken of in the same language.'

Occupy encampments around the world were subject to regular purges under the auspices of protecting sanitation and public health. In New York, the Occupy Wall Street camp in Zuccotti Park was cleared out after Brookfield Office Properties, the park's private owner, complained that the park hadn't been subject to its daily cleaning for a month. October through December 2011 saw a regular back-and-forth between the protesters and city officials, as the park was cleaned and subsequently reoccupied several times. Many sites were bulldozed to the ground. Ostensibly, the protesters were allowed to return, but their camps would inevitably be bulldozed again under similar justifications. Occupy Oakland itself was fully removed from both parks it had inhabited by mid-November 2011.

Calling the encampments fire or disease hazards absolved city officials and law enforcement of the otherwise-damaging PR hit of shutting down a movement with considerable popular support. The rhetoric of the 99 percent was catching on, and high-profile actors, musicians and activists were speaking to Occupy encampments around the world. To halt the encampments, Occupy had to be criminalized, and hygiene was the chosen method of control. Free speech and free assembly were held up against public well-being, and came up wanting.

The technico-medical apparatus exists to normalize the population under surveillance. Just as the workshop controls a person's time, and the cell isolates her body within a particular space, the hospital is a space where the unacceptable body is made normal. Bodies are governed using this apparatus; they are made healthy where they had been sick. But the cure doesn't have to heal a physical ailment. In Foucault, the hospital can stand in for any organization that seeks to change elements of a person's personality. So the rehabilitation model in prisons could be considered part of the technico-medical apparatus, as it is intended to alter the prisoner's behaviour to prevent recidivism. It will 'cure' her of her criminality.

Between the downtown sites of Occupy Oakland's encampments and the Port of Oakland lies Interstate 880, the Nimitz Freeway. Beneath that elevated highway is a sort of carceral complex of buildings: police, court, city jail and bail bonds offices strung along between 6th and 7th streets form a physical barrier between the concerns of the port and the concerns of the city. In the militarized city, the economy must be allowed to continue unabated, and the engines of moneymaking should be protected from the messiness of political protest.

As for Bentham, he was insistent that the public should be allowed to watch the workings of the Panopticon. In this case, the public's input did – eventually – reduce the planned scope of the DAC back to its original port-only focus. But it took more than two years of constant agitation and lobbying of the Oakland city council to ensure that scale-back. As with the Ring of Steel, public opinion is vital. A balance must be struck between the perceptions of safety and paranoia. For the creators of the Ring of Steel, displacement of criminal or terrorist activity was a major problem. If crime wasn't happening in the City anymore, it might just be pushed to other areas. This is why its boundaries were expanded later. But if you cover an entire city, that problem — at least for that city's elected administrators — is solved.

Panopticon Valley

There are times when Bentham's work on the Panopticon gives off a strong odour of 'crank.' The letters swing wildly from big ideas and hand-waving to obsessive concern with minutiae. When he's explaining the overall layout of the building, he leaves it in the hands of architects to work out what materials will allow the shape he has in mind, but then later he spends several pages working out a system of gears and tubes that would allow jailers to speak and signal to their charges with voice- and remote-operated flags.

Bentham's uneven obsessiveness reminds us of Steve Jobs. Notoriously detail-oriented, Jobs famously spent considerable time, for example, ensuring the scroll bars in OSX worked the way he wanted, or having opinions about and specifying the precise number of screws in a laptop case. All while he was best known publicly for his big pronouncements about the future of computing.

Jobs was quite secretive, but his competitors have plenty of Benthamite opinions about surveillance. See if you can spot the difference between Eric Schmidt, Mark Zuckerberg and Jeremy Bentham:

- If you have something that you don't want anyone to know, maybe you shouldn't be doing it in the first place, but if you really need that kind of privacy, the reality is that search engines including Google do retain this information for some time, and it's important, for example, that we are all subject in the United States to the Patriot Act. It is possible that that information could be made available to the authorities.

- The days of you having a different image for your work friends or co-workers and for the other people you know are probably coming to an end pretty quickly... Having two identities for yourself is an example of a lack of integrity.
- Supposing myself to have no forbidden enterprise in view, nor while I forbore such enterprises any abuse of power to apprehend, the idea of an inspector's presence would in the one case be a matter of indifference in the other case even of comfort.

One of the major differences between Bentham and these titans of industry, of course, is that they had full access to deep pockets, whereas he struggled to get financial support for his ideas. Is it possible that the fine line between a brilliant designer and a crank might just be defined by adequate financing? After all, though Bentham's exact design was never built, it was an early conceptual success in disruptive crowdsourcing for a notoriously labour-intensive industry.

'The panoptic mechanism arranges spatial unities that make it possible to see constantly and to recognize immediately. In short, it reverses the principle of the dungeon; or rather of its three functions — to enclose, to deprive of light and to hide — it preserves only the first and eliminates the other two. Full lighting and the eye of a supervisor capture better than darkness, which ultimately protected. Visibility is a trap.'

— Michel Foucault, *Discipline & Punish*

'I hope no critic of more learning than candour will do an inspection-house so much injustice as to compare it to *Dionysius' ear*. The object of that contrivance was, to know what prisoners said without their suspecting any such thing. The object of the inspection principle is directly the reverse: it is to make them not only *suspect*, but be *assured*, that whatever they do is known, even though that should not be the case. Detection is the object of the first: *prevention*, that of the latter. In the former case the ruling person is a spy; in the latter he is a monitor. The object of the first was to pry into the secret recesses of the heart; the latter, confining its attention to *overt acts*, leaves thoughts and fancies to their proper *ordinary*, the court *above*.'

— Jeremy Bentham, *Panopticon; or,*
The Inspection-House

We both happen to use iPhones. Tim bought his iPhone 4 in April 2011. Emily bought her iPhone 4S that November. Emily's phone is locked to a specific carrier. Tim's was bought unlocked. On the back of each, it says in silver type, 'Designed by Apple in California. Assembled in China.'

Making and selling an iPhone takes a tremendous amount of discipline. Apple's 2014 Supplier List – accounting for 97 percent of its procurement spending – counts two hundred separate entities. These are spread across every continent. Tracking efforts reach all the way back to minerals extracted from the earth where Apple is working to get its suppliers' suppliers to ensure they aren't buying from groups that 'finance or benefit armed groups that are associated with human rights violations.' Most entities on the list make some material or component that is eventually assembled in a factory in China (not all of the two hundred suppliers are necessarily involved in iPhone production). The vast supply network is made possible by Apple's own set of logistics and transportation disciplines, which in turn are made possible by the intermodal shipping container.

As our phones announce, they were both assembled in China – notoriously, by employees of Foxconn Technology Group, whose clients include a significant portion of contemporary electronics brands. The conditions at Foxconn iPhone-assembly factories in China's Special Economic Zones have been well-documented: workers sleep in crowded dormitories, work is repetitive and safety nets now ring the factories, a response to a series of suicides in 2010. The hours are long, and workers' rights groups claim that the corporate culture is oppressive and militaristic. As with any job involving an assembly line, breaks are few and rigorously controlled.

The 2010 suicides intensified the debate about whether working conditions violated labour law and reasonable labour practices. Foxconn's work environment came under more intense scrutiny from the national and international media. Apple hired an independent watchdog to audit the organization. The Supplier List is part of a larger Supplier Responsibility Report that relays Apple's efforts to ensure its suppliers are compliant with rules and regulations. For our purposes, this is irrelevant. A nice factory is still a factory, and Foxconn's labourers work very hard indeed. It is a highly disciplined environment. The response to too much discipline was another layer of discipline to keep the first layer in check. The watchers are being watched.

We are being watched as well. This is a side effect of the proper functioning of our phones. In 2011, security researchers Alasdair Allan and Pete Warden discovered that you could extract a file from an iPhone that contained a bunch of location data. The file, designed to speed up location look-up, maintained a cached database of Wi-Fi hot spots and cell towers. Which, given that it would make no sense to cache locations never visited, could be used to get a pretty good idea of where you'd been.

Apple has since changed the behaviour of the processes that generated this particular file, but it's one of the dozens, if not hundreds, of species of data exhaust that our devices throw off in the course of normal operation. Some files are simply temporary memory designed to improve responsiveness. Some files are diagnostic data, designed to help track down the source of software error. Some are the numbers, words, sounds and images we create by interacting with our devices. There are log files generated by activities on the phones and on the servers of our service providers and the websites we visit and the servers that sit between us at them. Some of the files are generated by processes working as intended. Some are generated by bugs. Some are working as intended, but turn out to be more revealing than originally planned.

A great deal of that information can be very valuable to the companies that provide many of the services we use on our phones. Emily uses her phone to access Facebook. Tim does not. Facebook is a billion-dollar company that makes its living by selling advertisers an opportunity to show ads to people like Emily (or to people not like Emily, depending on their demographic goals). We should not pick on Facebook here – a substantial proportion of contemporary content and service providers are supported by an advertising model that relies on an increasingly granular understanding of who we strangers are. In 2012, journalist Alexis Madrigal counted 105 trackers that picked up his scent over a thirty-six-hour period of ordinary web surfing. 'Every move you make on the Internet is worth some tiny amount to someone, and a panoply of companies want to make sure that no step along your Internet journey goes unmonetized,' he writes in *The Atlantic*. Google, which we both use, offers an editable but automatically generated profile to help us understand what advertisers see in us. Among the 206 interests it currently lists for Tim are: American Football (only a little), Beauty Pageants (not at all), Intelligence & Counterterrorism (yes).

In early June 2013, journalists Glenn Greenwald and Laura Poitras began to publish revelations from National Security Agency whistleblower Edward Snowden. Snowden had worked for the CIA as well as some of the NSA's private subcontractors. As part of his work, he had found evidence of global surveillance networks, including bulk surveillance of electronic communications. Here is the NSA's 'collection posture' as reported by Greenwald from a 2011 PowerPoint slide included in Snowden's trove of documents: 'Collect it All,' 'Process it All,' 'Exploit it All,' 'Partner it All,' 'Sniff it All' and 'Know it All.'

Panopticism. Now?

It seems to go without saying that the panopticon is ubiquitous, both within institutions and without. After all, we've just spent a whole book finding examples of panoptic spaces. But is the disciplinary regime Foucault described in *Discipline & Punish* really the right prism for examining our contemporary situation?

The panopticon is a child of a particular time. It was conceived by Bentham at the dawn of the Age of Industry and reinterpreted by Foucault at the dawn of the Age of Information. It's an industrial institution, created for factories, redesigned for incarceration and then adapted for everything. The disciplinary society that Foucault describes requires constant and minute attention. The trick of the panopticon is that you think you are being watched even when no one is watching. The cops are in your head. But they can only stay in your head with a lot of cunningly crafted policies and environmental affordances. The panopticon requires isolation, and isolation is in short supply in these networked times.

Foucault himself moved on from the conception of discipline. In the late 1970s, he gave a series of lectures at the Collège de France that were published in English as *Security, Territory, Population* and *The Birth of Biopolitics*. In these lectures, he expanded upon and further developed his work on discipline as well as his research into the histories of sexuality and madness. Most relevant to us is his reworking of the ideas of security (which he later reframed as 'governmentality') as a replacement for the disciplinary society he'd described in 1975.

While discipline requires enclosure, security is diffuse. Discipline seeks to eradicate even the smallest infraction; security seeks equilibrium. Only those most serious violations are pursued by the authorities. This is a means of governance with limits built in. Foucault's later work extended his idea of power – it's not just in institutions, it's in individuals, too.

How, then, to understand our smartphones? They seem to be intensifiers.

Smartphones can operate as vectors of surveillance and counter-surveillance. They are tools that allow corporations, governments and individuals to watch over the details of our lives, but they also allow us to watch right back. Our phones connect us to the network, which makes us collection points for data compilation. Mobile phones allow surveillance to be mutual, which is what Foucault predicted, particularly in his later work. Power operates multidirectionally, not simply from above. We watch, we are watched and we watch each other.

Smartphones enable exactly the kind of interconnectivity that Bentham designed his panopticon to avoid. We are not prevented from communicating with one another as his prisoners were, but our communications are tracked and monitored.

In the early days of the internet there was a great deal of excitement about that first part – the peer-to-peer connections, the ability to speak and be heard outside of the more industrial and hierarchical structures, the free flow of information, unlocking the global brain, etc. If that excitement hasn't faded entirely, it has been dulled by a growing understanding of the second part. Many of the apparent rebellious freedoms of the early internet were not technical features of the network but more a consequence of this new network being beneath the notice of power. It's not beneath notice anymore.

Columbia University professor Eben Moglen likens the situation to an ecological disaster resulting from rampant littering. No single piece of trash destroys an environment, but when everyone does it… 'The problem is caused by people who would like a little help spying on their friends. And in a genteel way, that's what the social media offers. They get to surveil other people. In return for a little bit of the product, they assist the growth of these immense commercial spying operations. The commercial spying operations are used to empower people who have lots to get more from people who have less.'

Moglen's analogy here isn't quite right. His focus on the social networks as an ecological disaster implies an otherwise pristine environment. This is hardly the case. Much of the intelligence and advertising community's collections activity involves telecoms that have little to do with social media. Our phones throw off plenty of alternate kinds of data exhaust through scraped e-mails, call metadata, warrantless wiretaps, search histories, server logs and advertising cookies.

And though it is convenient to conceive of 'power' as a monolith, it is not. Our phones are one user interface of the huge network that is required to make such surveillance possible. Global positioning satellites, RFID tags, drones and CCTV cameras are other physical points on this network, and a great deal more exists only in virtual space (i.e., vast warehouses of computation, located wherever power is cheap and/or internet is fast). This network is populated by a riot of factions and powers with interests sometimes aligned and sometimes at odds. In our very small way, we too are nodes in this network, watching and being watched.

Bentham designed the Panopticon as a machine to bring together a population fragmented by the industrial revolution. In *Discipline & Punish*, Foucault pointed out some of the problems with Enlightenment reforms. Thinkers like Bentham wanted to change things for the better, but they didn't always see the results of their actions. The short-term advantages of increased efficiency, the gathering of information about the population, and more humane punishments don't take into account the corrosive and destabilizing longer-term effects of continuous surveillance. In important ways, neither did the Foucault of 1975.

Writing for the *New Inquiry*, Steve Waldman contemplates the victory of Western capitalism over the command economies of the Soviet Union and its allies. 'Given the vast potential of an individual human body, it is astonishing how much control is exercised in the most ordinary of human actions and interactions,' he writes. 'The most unconventional or undisciplined people you will ever encounter still restrict their motions, facial expressions, behavior, and activity to an astonishingly narrow range of the possibilities of which their bodies [are] capable...

'[W]hen people claim that the "free market" system outproduced Soviet Communism, what they are saying is that markets more effectively produced discipline. It was more successful at imposing patterns of human action and restriction conducive to military and economic production than a command economy was capable of imposing.'

Global capitalism in turn gave us our iPhones.

In the End(s)

Bentham's *Panopticon* ends with a movement outward from the prison, as he imagines what other types of panoptic institutions might look like. He reasons that an ordinary factory wouldn't be so different from a prison factory. In madhouses, isolation would ensure no harm would come to others at the hands of an insane person (at the cost, perhaps, of rendering them more insane, but who's counting?). A panoptic hospital would allow patients to screen themselves from view when they liked, while remaining available to doctors. And, of course, a panoptic school would prevent cheating off one's neighbour's paper. The side benefit of such a school is that young girls could be transferred to one to preserve their virginities.

Bentham was not so foolish as to think good will would always come of panoptic institutions, for he believed them to be tools amenable to misuse like any other: 'If any perverse applications should ever be made of it, they will lie in this case as in others, at the doors of those who make them. Knives, however sharp, are very useful things, and, for most purposes, the sharper the more useful.' Bentham biographer Janet Semple brought attention to some of his more obscure panoptic flights of fancy, including a home for pregnant women in distress, a Panopticon Town and a moveable panopticon for hens.

Jeremy Bentham's plans to have a panoptic prison built came to nothing, though he tried to keep the British government interested in the scheme for over twenty years. War, bureaucracy and governmental inefficiency kept the prison from becoming realized, and as the eighteenth century wore into the nineteenth, enthusiasm for reformist plans waned. Even his *Panopticon* had fallen out of print until they were revived by Bentham's own utilitarian protege John Stuart Mill in 1816.

Foucault ends *Discipline & Punish* abruptly. He finishes his discussion of how the punishment systems of his day (and ours) came to be with an examination of the Mettray Penal Colony, opened in 1840, which he considers the apotheosis of the carceral system. All of the 'coercive technologies of behaviour' were brought to bear on the prisoner, who is gradually trained using the new science of psychology to become a productive member of society upon release. Foucault acknowledges that the ends are good – these various forces are supposed to cure people, to comfort them, to protect them – but that the power exercised tends to flatten the population, to normalize it. These are the forces that exist in the carceral city, too, but Foucault doesn't describe them in detail before finishing the book.

And how shall we end? Writing in 2011, John Berger suggests the best way to understand the current situation is to think of the entire world as a prison:

Michel Foucault has graphically shown how the penitentiary was a late eighteenth-, early nineteenth-century invention closely linked to industrial production, its factories and its utilitarian philosophy.

Earlier, there were jails that were extensions of the cage and the dungeon. What distinguished the penitentiary is the number of prisoners it can pack in – and the fact that all of them are under continuous surveillance thanks to the model of the Pantopticon, as conceived by Jeremy Bentham, who introduced the principle of accountancy into ethics.

Accountancy demands that every transaction be noted. Hence the penitentiary's circular walls with the cells arranged around the screw's watchtower at the center. Bentham, who was John Stuart Mill's tutor at the beginning of the nineteenth century, was the principal utilitarian apologist for industrial capitalism.

Today in the era of globalization, the world is dominated by financial, not industrial, capital, and the dogmas defining criminality and the logics of imprisonment have changed radically. Penitentiaries still exist and more and more are being built. But prison walls now serve a different purpose. What constitutes an incarceration area has been transformed.

Later, he considers the people around us.

They (we) are fellow prisoners. That recognition, in whatever tone of voice it may be declared, contains a refusal. Nowhere more than in prison is the future calculated and awaited as something utterly opposed to the present. The incarcerated never accept the present as final...

Between fellow prisoners there are conflicts, sometimes violent. All prisoners are deprived, yet there are degrees of deprivation and the differences of degree provoke envy. On this side of the walls life is cheap. The very facelessness of the global tyranny encourages hunts to find scapegoats, to find instantly definable enemies among other prisoners. The asphyxiating cells then become a madhouse. The poor attack the poor, the invaded pillage the invaded. Fellow prisoners should not be idealized.

Without idealization, simply take note that what they have in common — which is their unnecessary suffering, their endurance, their cunning — is more significant, more telling, than what separates them. And from this, new forms of solidarity are being born. The new solidarities start with the mutual recognition of differences and multiplicity. So this is life! A solidarity, not of masses but of interconnectivity, far more appropriate to the conditions of prison.

Here is the thing about Bentham: he really thought the Panopticon was going to help. He was genuine in his desire to make a better world, in the way that a lot of the utilitarians and enlightenment thinkers were. They thought they could plan it into existence.

Semple blames the creepy overtones of the panopticon project on Foucault and his bad attitude. His 'claustrophobic distrust of the world' makes him take this project that was a fundamentally hopeful thing and look at it the way we do now.

Reading this, we couldn't help but laugh. Sure, the problem with your scheme for 24/7 surveillance in a solitary-confinement—based forced-labour penitentiary system is that it got a bad rap from this French guy...

We wonder what Foucault would say to Semple.

I do indeed have a claustrophobic distrust of the world.

Have you not seen the world?

Which part of the world implies that you owe it more trust?

Sources

Bentham, Jeremy. *The Panopticon Writings*. Miran Bozovic, ed. London: Verso, 1995.

Foucault, Michel. *Discipline & Punish: The Birth of the Prison*. New York: Vintage Books, 1979.

Chapter 1

Bentham, Jeremy. *Deontology: or, The Science of Morality*. London: Longman, Rees, Orme, Browne, Green and Longman, 1834.

Brunon-Ernst, Anne. *Beyond Foucault: New Perspectives on Bentham's Panopticon*. Farnham: Ashgate, 2012.

Cieszkowski, Krzysztof Z. 'Millbank Before the Tate.' *The Tate Gallery Illustrated Biennial Report*, 1986.

Coelho, Alexandra Prado. 'O Pavilhão Maldito Que Sobrevive Escondido No Coração de Lisbo.' *Publico*: P2, 14 June 2009.

Cooper, Robert Alan. 'Jeremy Bentham, Elizabeth Fry, and English Prison Reform.' *Journal of the History of Ideas* 42:4, 1981.

Crampton, Jeremy W., and Stuart Elden. *Space, Knowledge and Power: Foucault and Geography*. Aldershot: Ashgate, 2007.

Cunningham, Peter. *The Hand-Book of London*. London: John Murray, 1850.

Dilts, Andrew and Bernard E. 'Harcourt Discipline, Security, and Beyond: A Brief Introduction.' *Carceral Notebooks* 4, 2008.

Dobson, Jerome E., and Peter F. Fischer. 'The Panopticon's Changing Geography.' *Geographical Review* 97:3, 2007.

'Dutch Open "Big Brother" jail.' *BBC News*, 19 January 2006.

'Edinburgh's Bridewell.' *Georgian Edinburgh*, 2 October 2011.

Higgins, Peter. 'The Scurvy Scandal at Millbank Penitentiary: A Reassessment.' *Medical History* 50:4, 2006.

Kennedy, Jane. 'Before Tate Britain, There Was the Dreaded Millbank Prison.' Tate Blog, 28 October 2013.

Kinghorn, Sandy. 'Edinburgh Bridewell: Influences.' The Architecture of Robert Adam 1728-1792 (online).

Miller, Jacques Allain, and Richard Miller. 'Jeremy Bentham's Panoptic Device.' *October* 41, 1987.

'Presidio Modelo in Cuba and the Panopticon Idea.' *dpr Barcelona* blog, 21 October 2009.

Rabinow, Paul, and Nikolas Rose. 'Foucault Today.' *The Essential Foucault: Selections from the Essential Works of Foucault, 1954–1984.* Rabinow and Rose, eds. New York: New Press, 2003.

'The Roundhouse History' (online).

Schiller, Nikolas. 'The Millbank Penitentiary, the Tate Britain, and the Panopticon.' *The Daily Render*, 26 July 2008.

Steadman, Philip. *Building Types and Built Forms* (Leicestershire: Matador, 2014).

'The St. Petersburg Panopticon.' UCL Bentham Project (online)

Wilson, David. 'Millbank, The Panopticon and Their Victorian Audiences.' *The Howard Journal*. 41:4, 2002.

Wolters, Eugene. 'The Mainstream Media Just Discovered Foucault and They're All Wrong.' Verso Blog, 30 July 2013.

Wood, David. 'Beyond the Panopticon? Foucault and Surveillance Studies,' in *Space, Knowledge and Power: Foucault and Geography,* ed. J. Crampton and S. Elden, Aldershot: Ashgate, 2007.

———. 'Foucault and Panopticism Revisited.' *Surveillance & Society* 1:3, 2003.

Chapter 2

'Behind These Walls.' Video produced by University of Oregon. 14 July 2010.

Bernstein, David. *The Use of Prison Labor: The Economic, Environmental, and Security Concerns.* AnythingII, 2013.

'Eastern Oregon Correctional Institution.' Oregon Government (online).

'Frequently Asked Questions.' The National Cotton Council of America (online).

Garvey, Stephen P. 'Freeing Prisoners' Labor.' *Stanford Law Review* 50:2, 1998.

Gilmore, Ruth Wilson. 'Globalisation and US Prison Growth: From Military Keynesianism to Post-Keynesian Militarism.' *Race and Class* 40:2/3, 1998-99.

Hawkins, Gordon. 'Prison Labor and Prison Industries.' *Crime and Justice* 5, 1983.

'Inmate Population Statistics.' Oregon Government (online).

Kiesling, Phil, et al. *Strategic Assessment of OCE/DOC Work and Related Programs: Phase I.* Portland: Center for Public Service, 2012.

———. *Strategic Assessment of OCE/DOC Work and Related Programs: Phase II.* Portland: Center for Public Service, 2012.

———. *Strategic Assessment of Oregon Corrections Enterprises (OCE): Phase II.* Portland: Center for Public Service, 2013.

Lichtenstein, Alex. *Twice the Work of Free Labor: The Political Economy of Convict Labor in the New South.* London: Verso, 1996

Mayeux, Sara. 'A Different Take on Prison Labor and the Thirteenth Amendment.' Prison Law Blog, 16 December 2010.

——— 'Prison Labor and the Thirteenth Amendment.' Prison Law Blog, 16 December 2010.

McDonald, John R. 'Federal Prison Industry Reform: The Demise of Prison Factories.' *Public Contract Law Journal* 35:4, 2006.

Millay, John R. 'From Asylum to Penitentiary: The Social Impact of Eastern Oregon Correctional Institution upon Pendleton.' *Humboldt Journal of Social Relations* 17:1/2, 1991.

'Oregon Corrections Enterprises.' Oregon Government (online).

'Oregon State Prison Inmates Required to Work Full Time, Measure 17 (1994).' Ballotpedia.org.

Oyangen, Knut. 'The Cotton Economy of the Old South.' *American Agricultural History Primer* (online).

Perkinson, Robert. *Texas Tough: The Rise of America's Prison Empire*. New York: Metropolitan, 2010.

Phillips, William H. 'Cotton Gin.' Economic History Association (online).

Raghunath, Raja. 'A Promise the Nation Cannot Keep: What Prevents the Application of the Thirteenth Amendment in Prison?' *William & Mary Bill of Rights Journal* 18:2, 2009.

Reynolds, Morgan O. *Factories Behind Bars*. Dallas: National Center for Policy Analysis, 1996.

Runyan-Gless, Jessica. 'Inside Story on Where Beds, Desks and Other Dorm Furniture Are Made.' KVAL.com, 29 October 2013.

'Spread of Cotton: 1790–1860.' The University of Oregon: Mapping History (online).

Stanziani, Alessandro. 'The Traveling Panopticon: Labor Institutions and Labor Practices in Russia and Britain in the Eighteenth and Nineteenth Centuries.' *Comparative Studies in Society and History* 51:4, 2009.

Thompson, Heather Ann. 'How Prisons Change the Balance of Power in America.' *The Atlantic*, 7 October 2013.

———. 'Rethinking Working-Class Struggle Through the Lens of the Carceral State: Toward a Labor History of Inmates and Guards.' *Labor: Studies in Working-Class History of the Americas* 8:3, 2011.

———. 'Why Mass Incarceration Matters: Rethinking Crisis, Decline, and Transformation in Postwar American History.' *The Journal of American History*, 2010.

Todd, William Andrew. 'Convict Lease System.' New Georgia Encyclopedia (online).

Wagner, Peter. T*he Prison Index: Taking the Pulse of the Crime Control Industry.* Northampton: Prison Policy Initiative, 2003.

Werret, Simon. 'The Panopticon in the Garden: Samuel Bentham's Inspection House and Noble Theatricality in 18th Century Russia.' *Ab Imperio* 3, 2008.

Werret, Simon. 'Potemkin and the Panopticon: Samuel Bentham and the Architecture of Absolutism in Eighteenth Century Russia.' *Journal of Bentham Studies* 2, 1999.

Young, Cynthia. 'Punishing Labor: Why Labor Should Oppose the Prison Industrial Complex.' *New Labor Forum* 7, 2000.

Zaitz, Les. 'Oregon Corrections Enterprises Needs Changes to Survive, PSU report says.' *The Oregonian*, 2 March 2013.

Chapter 3

Bradbury, Steven J. 'Memorandum for John A. Rizzo, Senior Deputy General Counsel, Central Intelligence Agency.' 10 May 2005.

———. 'Memorandum for John A. Rizzo, Senior Deputy General Counsel, Central Intelligence Agency.' 30 May 2005.

Crabapple, Molly. 'It Don't Gitmo Any Better Than This.' Vice.com, 31 July 2013.

———. 'No One Reads Kafka in Gitmo.' Medium.com, 15 September 2013.

'DOD News Briefing: Secretary Rumsfeld and Gen. Pace.' U.S. Department of Defense transcript, 22 January 2002.

Garamone, Jim. '50 Detainees Now at Gitmo: All Treated Humanely.' American Forces Press Service, 15 January 2002.

'Gitmo Files and Photos.' Cryptome.org, 13 April 2008.

'Guantanamo Bay Naval Base and Ecological Crises.' Trade and Environment Database (online).

'Guantanamo Ten Years On.' Human Rights Watch (online).

'A History of the Detainee Population.' *The New York Times*, 31 May 2014.

Hussain, Murtaza. 'Chronicle of a Death Foretold.' *Al Jazeera*, 22 September 2012.

'Interrogation/Torture and Dual Loyalty.' Institute on Medicine as a Profession (online).

Kristof, Nicholas D. 'Beating Specialist Baker.' *The New York Times*, 5 June 2004.

Lelyveld, Joseph. 'In Guantanamo.' *The New York Review of Books*, 7 November 2002.

Postel, Therese. 'How Guantanamo Bay's Existence Helps Al-Qaeda Recruit More Terrorists.' *The Atlantic*, 12 April 2013.

Rayment, Sean. 'Guantánamo Bay: Inside the Empty, Rotting 'Torture' Blocks of Camp X-Ray.' *The Telegraph*, 10 June 2012.

Recon: Inside the Wire at Guantanamo Bay, Cuba and Camp Delta. Documentary made by U.S. military.

Rosenberg, Carol v. U.S. Department of Defense, 'Memorandum of Points and Authorities in Support of the Department of Defense's Motion for Summary Judgement.' 31 January 2014.

Savage, Charlie, et al. 'Classified Files Offer New Insights into Detainees.' *The New York Times*, 24 April 2011.

'Soldiers Unite to Defend Camp X-Ray.' *The Telegraph*, 25 January 2002.

'The Torture Question.' *Frontline*, PBS television.

'US Tortured Camp X-Ray Suspects, Says Lawyer.' *The Scotsman*, 9 October 2003.

Yoo, John, and Robert J. Delahunty. 'Memorandum for William J. Haynes II General Counsel, Department of Defense.' 9 January 2002.

Chapter 4

Altiok, Tayfur, and Benjamin Melamed. 'Modeling VACIS Security Operations at NY/NJ Marine Terminals.' DIMACS–CAIT Laboratory for Port Security at Rutgers University, 2006.

'Annual Report FY 2008–2009.' The Waterfront Commission of New York Harbor, 2009.

'Annual Report FY 2009–2010.' The Waterfront Commission of New York Harbor, . 2010.

'Annual Report FY 2010–2011.' The Waterfront Commission of New York Harbor, 2011.

'Annual Report FY 2011–2012.' The Waterfront Commission of New York Harbor, 2012.

Berson, Alan D. 'Lines and Flows: The Beginning and End of Borders.' *World Customs Journal* 6:1, 2012.

Bliss, Jeff. 'U.S. Backs Off All-Cargo Scanning Goal with Inspections at 4%.' Bloomberg News, 13 August 2012.

'The Changing Face of Organized Crime in New Jersey: A Status Report.' State of New Jersey Commission of Investigation, May 2004.

Cirincione, R., A. Cosmas, C. Low, J. Peck, and J. Wilds. 'Barriers to the Success of 100% Maritime Cargo Container Scanning.' *Final Report, Introduction to Technology and Policy, Massachusetts Institute of Technology Engineering Systems Division, Massachusetts Institute of Technology*, Cambridge, MA, 2007.

Cone, Tracie. 'AP IMPACT: Foreign Insects, Diseases Got into U.S.' *Washington Times*, 10 October 2011.

Cowen, Deborah. 'Circulating Stuff: From Military Art to Business Science.' Talk, 2011.

———. 'A Geography of Logistics: Market Authority and the Security of Supply Chains.' *Annals of the Association of American Geographers* 100:3, 2010.

———. 'Struggling with "Security": National Security and Labour in the Ports.' *Just Labour: A Canadian Journal of Work and Society* 10, 2007.

Crist, Philippe. 'Security in Maritime Transport: Risk Factors and Economic Impact.' Report to OECD Maritime Transport Committee, July 2003.

'The Department of Homeland Security Seal.' Department of Homeland Security (online).

'Detecting Nuclear Weapons and Radiological Materials: How Effective Is Available Technology?' Joint Hearing Before the Subcommittee on Prevention of Nuclear and Biological Attack, 21 June 2005.

'Eyeballing the NYC Bronx–Port Morris Gas Facility.' Cryptome.org, 16 September 2004.

Finnegan, William. 'Watching the Waterfront.' *The New Yorker*, 12 July 2006.

Fisch, Joseph. 'Investigation of the Waterfront Commission of New York Harbor.' State of New York Office of the Inspector General, August 2009.

Fischer, James T. *On the Irish Waterfront: The Crusader, the Movie, and the Soul of the Port of New York*. Ithaca: Cornell University Press, 2009.

Franz, Douglas. 'Port Security: U.S. Fails to Meet Deadline for Scanning of Cargo Containers.' *The Washington Post*, 15 July 2012.

Frittelli, J. 'Port and Maritime Security: Background and Issues for Congress.' *Port and Maritime Security* 11, 2008.

Hesketh, David. 'Weaknesses in the Supply Chain: Who Packed the Box?' *World Customs Journal* 4:2, September 2010.

Huizenga, D. 'Detecting Nuclear Weapons and Radiological Materials: How Effective Is Available Technology? Testimony Before the Subcommittee on Prevention of Nuclear and Biological Attacks and the Subcommittee on

Emergency Preparedness.' *Science and Technology, The House Commmittee on Homeland Security*, 2005.

'The Humble Hero: Containers Have Been More Important for Globalisation Than Freer Trade.' *The Economist*, 18 May 2013.

Maritime Transport Committee. 'Security in Maritime Transport: Risk Factors and Economic Impact.' *Organisation for Economic Co-operation and Development* 14, 2003.

McGeehan, Patrick. 'No-Show Jobs and Overstaffing Hurt New York Harbor, a Report Says.' *The New York Times*, March 21, 2012.

Malyshenko, Yuri V. 'Completeness, Correctness and Reliability of Customs Control.' *World Customs Journal* 7:1, 2013.

Medalia, Jonathan. 'Port and Maritime Security: Potential for Terrorist Nuclear Attack Using Oil Tankers.' CRS Report for Congress, 2004.

Natsios, Deborah. 'New York Voir Dire: Interrogating the Juridical City State of Exception.' Cryptome.org, 1 February 2012.

Nguyen, Tranq. 'Changes to the Role of US Customs and Border Protection and the Impact of 100% Container Scanning Law.' *World Customs Journal*, 2012.

Parlette, Vanessa, and Deborah Cowen. 'Dead Malls: Suburban Activism, Local Spaces, Global Logistics.' *International Journal of Urban and Regional Research* 35.4, 2011.

Pellegrini, Frank. 'The Bush Speech: How to Rally a Nation.' *Time*, 21 September 2001.

Peterson, Joann, and Alan Treat. 'The Post-9/11 Global Framework for Cargo Security.' U.S. International Trade Commission, *Journal of International Commerce and Economics*, 2008.

'Port Security Hearing.' Subcommittee of the U.S. Senate Committee on Appropriations, 4 April 2002 (online).

Rosenzweig, Paul. '100% Scanning of Cargo.' Lawfare blog, 16 July 2012.

'Safety and Security Zones: New York Marine Inspection Zone and Captain of the Port Zone.' Cryptome.org, 19 February 2003.

Sequeira, Sandra, and Simeon Djankov. 'On the Waterfront: An Empirical Study of Corruption in Ports.' Harvard University, December 2008.

'SCI 33rd Annual Report.' State of New Jersey Commission of Investigation, 2001.

'SCI 34th Annual Report.' State of New Jersey Commission of Investigation, 2002.

'SCI 45th Annual Report.' State of New Jersey Commission of Investigation, 2013.

'Talking Points on Requiring 100% Container Scanning at Overseas Ports.' American Association of Port Authorities, 23 August 2010.

Traspani, Lorraine. 'Trade Risk Management: A Global Approach.' *World Customs Journal* 6:2, September 2012.

'What Is VACIS Exam in US Import Customs Clearance.' HowtoImport Export.com, 3 June 2013.

Chapter 5

Basulto, David. 'US Embassy in London / KieranTimberlake Architects.' *Arch Daily*, 24 February 2010.

Bridle, James. 'How Britain Exported Next-Generation Surveillance.' Medium.com, 18 December 2013.

Brown, Patricia Leigh. 'Ideas & Trends: Designs for a Land Of Bombs and Guns.' *The New York Times*, 28 May 1995.

Buchan, Bruce, and David Ellison. 'Speaking to the Eye.' *Cultural Studies Review* 18:3, 2012.

Coaffee, Jon. 'Rings of Steel, Rings of Concrete and Rings of Confidence: Designing out Terrorism in Central London Pre and Post September 11th.' *International Journal of Urban and Regional Research* 28:1, 2004.

———. *Terrorism, Risk and the Global City: Towards Urban Resilience*. Farnham: Ashgate, 2009.

'CPTED for Dense Commercial Settings.' Portland Oregon Government, October 2009 (online).

Davis, Mike. *Beyond Blade Runner: Urban Control The Ecology of Fear.* Open Magazine Pamphlet Series, 1992.

Deleuze, Gilles. 'Postscript on the Societies of Control.' *October* 59, 1992.

DMJM H+N. 'Blast-Resistant Facilities: Even Terrorists Can't Break The Laws of Physics.' *American City & County*, 1 February 2004.

'FEMA 430, Site and Urban Design for Security: Guidance Against Potential Terrorist Attacks.' Federal Emergency Management Agency, 2007 (online).

Flatow, Nicole. 'Police Are Using License Plate Readers to Track Your Car's Movements.' *Think Progress*, 27 June 2013.

'Fortress Urbanism.' *BBC Culture Show*, 17 May 2011.

Giblin, Kelly A. 'The Jersey Barrier.' *American Heritage* 22:1, 2006.

Graham, Stephen. 'Foucault's Boomerang: The New Military Urbanism.' *Open Democracy*, 14 February 2013.

Hutchinson, Sean. 'Why Are Road Partitions Called Jersey Barriers?' *Mental Floss*, 10 July 2013.

Johnson, Bobbie. 'Going Inside the Ring of Steel.' Medium.com, 25 September 2013.

Kelly, Owen. 'The IRA Threat to the City of London.' Internet Law Book Reviews (online).

KieranTimberlake. 'Winning Design Concept.' U.S. Embassy press release, 23 February 2010 (online).

Koskela, Hille. '"Cam Era" – the contemporary urban Panopticon.' *Surveillance & Society* 1:3, 2003.

Kozel, Scott M. 'New Jersey Median Barrier History.' Roads to the Future (online).

Mann, Charles C. 'Smoke Screening.' *Vanity Fair*, 20 December 2011.

Mathieson, S. A. 'Britain's Secret Police.' Medium.com, 5 September 2013.

McCahill, Michael, and Clive Norris. *CCTV in London*. Hull: Centre for Criminology and Criminal Justice, 2002.

McDonald, Henry. 'Northern Ireland Police Chief Warns of Dissident Attacks in Run-up to Christmas.' *The Guardian*, 25 November 2013.

McKittrick, David. 'Belfast Security Measures Accepted as Normal: People in Belfast Have Become Accustomed to Police Checks and the "Ring of Steel" Which Protects the City's Commercial Heart.' *The Independent*, 7 December 1992.

Molotch, Harvey, and Noah McClain. 'Dealing with Urban Terror: Heritages of Control, Varieties of Intervention, Strategies of Research.' *International Journal of Urban and Regional Research* 27:3, 2003.

Natsios, Deborah. 'Voir Dire: Interrogating NYC's Ring of Steel.' Cryptome.org, 13 July 2012.

Newman, Oscar. *Creating Defensible Space*. U.S. Department of Housing and Urban Development, 1996.

Ouroussoff, Nicolai. 'A New Fort, er, Embassy, for London.' *The New York Times*, 23 February 2010.

'Recommended Security Guidelines for Airport Planning, Design and Construction.' Transportation Security Administration, 15 June 2006 (online).

'"Ring of Steel" Widened.' *BBC News*, 18 December 2003.

Schell, Terry L., et al. 'Designing Airports for Security: An Analysis of Proposed Changes at LAX.' RAND Corporation, 2003 (online).

Schienke, Erich W., and Bill Brown. 'Streets into Stages: An Interview with Surveillance Camera Players' Bill Brown.' *Surveillance & Society* 1:3, 2003.

Yar, Majid. 'Panoptic Power and the Pathologisation of Vision: Critical Reflections on the Foucauldian Thesis.' *Surveillance & Society* 1:3, 2003.

Chapter 6

Adams, Jane Meredith. 'U.S. Foils Major Smuggling Operation Chinese Gunrunners Caught in Sting.' *Chicago Tribune*, 24 May 1996.

Anderson, George et al. 'Organized Crime in California, 2007-2008' (online).

Armitage, Rachel. *To CCTV or Not to CCTV?: A Review of Current Research into the Effectiveness of CCTV Systems in Reducing Crime*. London: Nacro Crime and Social Policy Section, 2002.

Artz, Matthew. 'Oakland Police Department Avoids Federal Takeover, But Agrees to Unprecedented Control Over Police.' *SFGate*, 6 December 2012.

Bond-Graham, Darwin, and Ali Winston. 'The Real Purpose of Oakland's Surveillance Center.' *East Bay Express*, 18 December 2013.

Bulwa, Demian. 'Police Spies Chosen to Lead War Protest.' *SFGate*, 28 July 2006.

Cagle, Susie. 'The Testing Ground for the New Surveillance.' Medium.com, 18 February 2014.

City of Oakland. 'Agenda Report to Deanna J. Santana.' 23 June 2013 (online).

CNN Staff. 'Cities Struggle to Deal with Occupy Movement.' CNN.com, 15 November 2011.

Conan, Neal, et al. 'Occupy Wall Street: The Future And History, So Far.' *Talk of the Nation*, National Public Radio, 9 February 2012.

'Crime Rate in Oakland, California (CA).' City-data.com (online).

Gill, Martin, and Angela Spriggs. *Assessing the Impact of CCTV*. London: Home Office Research, Development and Statistics Directorate, 2005.

'The Federal Bureau of Investigation's Efforts to Protect the Nation's Seaports.' U.S. Department of Justice Audit Division, March 2006 (online).

Finoki, Bryan, Nick Sowers, and Javier Arbona. 'A Weaponized Urbanity: Morning Drift in Militarized Downtown Oakland.' Podcast recorded May 2, 2014.

Flynn, Steven, et al. *America Still Unprepared – America Still in Danger*. Council on Foreign Relations, 2002.

Hall, Peter V. '"We'd Have to Sink the Ships": Impact Studies and the 2002 West Coast Port Lockout.' *Economic Development Quarterly* 18:4, 2004.

Haveman, Jon D., and Howard J. Shatz, eds. *Protecting the Nation's Seaports: Balancing Security and Cost*. San Francisco: Public Policy Institute of California, 2006.

Haveman, Jon D., Howard J. Shatz, and Ernesto Vilchis. 'An Overview of Port Security Programs.' PowerPoint presentation, Public Policy Institute of California and Princeton University, 21–22 August 2004.

Heiner, Brady Thomas. 'Foucault and the Black Panthers.' City 11:3, 2007.

Isnard, Adrienne. *Can Surveillance Cameras Be Successful in Preventing Crime and Controlling Anti-Social Behaviours?* Australian Institute of Criminology, 2001.

Jones, Dewitt, ed. *History of the Port of Oakland: 1850–1934*. Works Progress Administration (online).

Kane, Will. 'Oakland Cops Aim to Scrap Gunfire-Detecting ShotSpotter.' *SFGate*, 14 March 2014.

King, Mike. 'Disruption Is Not Permitted: The Policing and Social Control of Occupy Oakland.' *Critical Criminology* 21, 2013.

Klein, Allison. 'Police Go Live Monitoring D.C. Crime Cameras.' *Washington Post*, 11 February 2008 .

Kuruvila, Matthai. 'Oakland Burglaries Barely Investigated.' *SFGate*, 9 May 2013.

Mahler, Jonathan. 'Oakland, the Last Refuge of Radical America.' *The New York Times*, 1 August 2012.

Mosendz, Polly. 'Chicago Gets a New Surveillance System Straight Out of a Video Game.' *The Atlantic Wire*, 24 June 2014.

Norton, Quinn. 'A Eulogy for Occupy.' *Wired*, 12 December 2012.

Oakland Police Department. 'An Informational Report from the Chief of Police Detailing the Department's Ability, Strategy, and Plan for the Use of Surveillance Cameras Throughout the City of Oakland, Including Partnerships with Merchants and Other Agencies.' Memo, 8 July 2008 (online).

———. 'Training Bulletin.' 28 October 2005 (online).

'Oakland Residents Tell City: "Stop the Spy Center."' *Al Jazeera* staff, 19 February 2014.

Phillips, Coretta. 'A Review of CCTV Evaluations: Crime Reduction Effects and Attitudes Toward Its Use.' *Crime Prevention Studies* 10, 1999.

'Port of Oakland Documents Show More Questionable Spending of Public Funds.' KVTU.com, 31 March 2013.

'Port of Oakland History.' Port of Oakland (online).

Ratcliffe, Jerry. 'Video Surveillance of Public Places.' *Problem-Oriented Guides for Police Response Guides Series*, Community Oriented Policing Services, U.S. DoJ, February 2006.

Rosen, Eva, and Sudhir Venkatesh. 'Legal Innovation and the Control of Gang Behavior.' *Annual Review of Law and Social Science*, 2007.

Rosen, Rebecca J. 'London Riots, Big Brother Watches: CCTV Cameras Blanket the U.K.' *The Atlantic*, 9 August 2011.

Sanger, David E., and Steven Greenhouse. 'President Invokes Taft-Hartley Act to Open 29 Ports.' *The New York Times*, 9 October 2002.

Smith, Greg B. 'Behind the Smoking Guns: Inside NYPD's 21st Century Arsenal.' *The New York Daily News*.

'South Field Oakland Airport and the Jet Age' Vide, by W. A. Palmer, 1962.

Surveillance Studies Centre. 'FAQs about Camera Surveillance.' Queen's University (online).

Swaine, Jon. 'New York Settles with Occupy Wall Street Demonstrators.' *The Guardian*, 10 June 2014.

Taylor, Sunaura. 'Occupy Oakland.' *n + 1*, 27 October 2011.

'Terrorism in the United States.' FBI Counterterrorism Report, 1999 (online).

'Thousands Join Anti-War Movement.' BBC News, 1967 (online).

Vaidya, Aditi. 'Clean Air, Good Jobs: Green-Brown Alliance for Worker and Community Rights.' *Race, Poverty & the Environment* 16:1, 2009.

Winston, Ali. 'The Police Raid on Occupy Oakland Was Nothing New for This City.' ColorLines.com, 28 October 2011.

Zetter, Kim. 'Feds' Use of Fake Cell Tower: Did It Constitute a Search?' *Wired*, 3 November 2011.

Chapter 7

'Apple Q&A on Location Data' Apple.com, 27 April 2011.

Berger, John. 'Fellow Prisoners.' *Guernica*, 15 July 2011.

Bowcott, Owen. 'Social Media Mass Surveillance Is Permitted by Law, Says Top UK Official.' *The Guardian*, 17 June 2014.

boyd, danah, 'Dear Voyeur, meet Flâneur…Sincerely, Social Media,' *Surveillance & Society*, 8:4 (2011).

———. 'Facebook's Privacy Trainwreck: Exposure, Invasion, and Social Convergence.' *Convergence: The International Journal of Research into New Media Technologies*, 2008.

Chen, Jacqui. 'How Apple Tracks Your Location Without Consent, and Why It Matters.' *Ars Technica*, 20 April 2011.

Cohen, Nicole S. 'The Valorization of Surveillance: Towards a Political Economy of Facebook.' *Democratic Communique* 22:1, 2008.

Crawford, Kate. 'The Anxieties of Big Data.' *The New Inquiry*, 30 May 2014.

Doctorow, Cory. 'Ukraine Government Sends Text to Protesters: "Dear Subscriber, You Are Registered as a Participant in a Mass Disturbance."' *BoingBoing*, 23 January 2014.

'Facebook Law Enforcement Guidelines.' Facebook.com, 2010.

Felten, Ed. 'On the Ethics of A/B Testing.' *Freedom to Tinker* blog, 8 July 2014.

Felten, Edward W. 'ACLU Affidavit.' U.S. District Court, Southern N.Y., 26 August 2013.

Flatow, Nicole. 'How Officials Are Using Border Security to Justify Invasive Searches of Electronic Devices.' ThinkProgress.com, 10 September 2013.

Foucault, Michel. *The Birth of Biopolitics: Lectures at the Collège de France 1978–79*, Graham Burchell, trans. London: Palgrave Macmillan, 2008.

Freeze, Colin. 'Canada's Spy Agencies Chastised for Duping Courts.' *The Globe and Mail*, 20 December 2013.

Glenn, Joshua. 'The Black Iron Prison.' *Hilobrow*, 13 July 2011.

Goldstein, Harry. 'We Like to Watch.' IEEE Spectrum, 1 July 2004 (online).

Jain, Anab. 'Valley of the Meatpuppets.' *Superflux*, 29 June 2014.

Jeffries, Adrianne. 'In Which Eben Moglen Like, Legit Yells at Me for Having Facebook.' *Beta Beat*, 13 December 2011.

Johnson, Joel. '1 Million Workers. 90 Million iPhones. 17 Suicides. Who's to Blame?' *Wired*, 28 February 2011.

Madrigal, Alexis. 'How Much Is Your Data Worth? Mmm, Somewhere Between Half a Cent and $1,200.' *The Atlantic*, 19 March 2012.

———. 'I'm Being Followed: How Google – and 104 Other Companies – Are Tracking Me on the Web.' *The Atlantic*, 29 February 2012.

McGarry, Bill. 'How to Find Your Suspect's Facebook Profile If They Have Changed Their Username or Contact Details.' Toronto Police Service, 23 September 2013.

'Publicly Available Social Media Monitoring and Situational Awareness Initiative Update.' Department of Homeland Security, 6 January 2011.

Sanchez, Julian. 'Snowden Showed Us Just How Big the Panopticon Really Was. Now It's Up to Us.' *The Guardian*, 5 June 2014.

Semple, Janet. *Bentham's Prison: A Study of the Panopticon Penitentiary*. Oxford: Clarendon Press, 1993.

Surowiecki, James. ' How Steve Jobs Changed.' *The New Yorker*, 17 October 2011.

Timm, Trevor. 'The Surveillance State Can't Even Keep Track of How Many People It's Spying on Anymore. Time to Close the Loopholes.' *The Guardian*, 2 July 2014.

Tufecki, Zeynep. 'Is the Internet Good or Bad? Yes.' Medium.com, 12 February 2014.

Waldman, Steve Randy. 'No Choice But Freedom.' *The New Inquiry*, 1 May 2014.

Weimann, Gabriel. New Terrorism and New Media. Washington, D.C.: Commons Lab of the Woodrow Wilson International Center for Scholars, 2014.

Weir, Bill. 'A Trip to The iFactory: "Nightline" Gets an Unprecedented Glimpse Inside Apple's Chinese Core.' ABC News, 20 February 2012.

Zhang, Chi-Chi. 'Apple Manufacturing Plant Workers Complain of Long Hours, Militant Culture.' CNN, 6 February 2012.

Acknowledgements

We'd like to thank everyone at Coach House for being excited about editing and publishing this thing. In particular, Jason McBride, Stuart Ross and Alana Wilcox for their editing work at various stages from rough overview to final fiddly details.

Our partners Corey Ponder and Pamela Shapiro provided much support, advice and patience during the writing process. Then, on very short notice, they joined Matthew Battles, Amy Johnson, Justin Pickard, Eleanor Saitta, Sara Watson and some anonymous friends to pore over the completed draft. Thank you all; the book is much stronger for your comments.

Tim benefited a great deal from his time with metaLAB and the Berkman community at large this semester. Emily was a rogue scholar. We gratefully acknowledge the Access Copyright Foundation, who supported the production of this book with a research grant, and the Ontario Arts Council, who gave us a Writers' Reserve grant.

Making a list of all the people whose work has transformed yours is a fool's game, but we're going to try anyway. Here are some people whose work particularly influenced our approach to this topic: James Bridle, Debbie Chachra, Deb Cowen, Molly Crabapple, Marc Levinson, Geoff Manaugh, Roman Mars, Nicholas de Monchaux, Quinn Norton, Adam Rothstein, Elleanor Saitta and Nicola Twilley.

Lastly, we'd like to thank our parents for their years of support, the Border Town participants for reinvigorating our love (?) of surveillance and the University of King's College for introducing us, putting Foucault in our hands and having faculty who allowed us to write joint papers every chance we got.

Emily Horne lives and works in Toronto, Ontario. She is the photographer and designer for the webcomic *A Softer World*, and freelance edits books for kicks. Her work has appeared in *The Guardian*, *The Coast* and Tor.com. She is @birdlord on Twitter.

Tim Maly writes about design, architecture, networks and infrastructure. He is a fellow at Harvard's metaLAB and is big into cyborgs. His work has appeared in *Wired*, *Medium*, *The Atlantic* and Urban Omnibus. He is @doingitwrong on Twitter.

About the
Exploded Views Series

Exploded Views is a series of probing, provocative essays that offer surprising perspectives on the most intriguing cultural issues and figures of our day. Longer than a typical magazine article but shorter than a full-length book, these are punchy salvos written by some of North America's most lyrical journalists and critics. Spanning a variety of forms and genres — history, biography, polemic, commentary — and published simultaneously in all digital formats and handsome, collectible print editions, this is literary reportage that at once investigates, illuminates and intervenes.

www.chbooks.com/explodedviews

Typeset in Goodchild Pro and Gibson Pro. Goodchild was designed by Nick Shinn in 2002 at his ShinnType foundry in Orangeville, Ontario. Shinn's design takes its inspiration from French printer Nicholas Jenson who, at the height of the Renaissance in Venice, used the basic Carolingian minuscule calligraphic hand and classic roman inscriptional capitals to arrive at a typeface that produced a clear and even texture that most literate Europeans could read. Shinn's design captures the calligraphic feel of Jensen's early types in a more refined digital format. Gibson was designed by Rod McDonald in honour of John Gibson FGDC (1928–2011), Rod's long-time friend and one of the founders of the Society of Graphic Designers of Canada. It was McDonald's intention to design a solid, contemporary and affordable sans serif face.

Printed at the old Coach House on bpNichol Lane in Toronto, Ontario, on Rolland Opaque Natural paper, which was manufactured, acid-free, in Saint-Jérôme, Quebec, from 50 percent recycled paper, and it was printed with vegetable-based ink on a 1965 Heidelberg KORD offset litho press. Its pages were folded on a Baumfolder, gathered by hand, bound on a Sulby Auto-Minabinda and trimmed on a Polar single-knife cutter.

Edited by Jason McBride
Copy edited by Stuart Ross
Designed by Alana Wilcox
Series cover design by Ingrid Paulson
Cover photo: *F-House #1, Stateville Correctional Center, Illinois, 2010*, by David Leventi. Courtesy of the Bau-Xi Gallery.
Photo of Emily Horne by Jeremy Wike
Photo of Tim Maly by Kate Beaton

Coach House Books
80 bpNichol Lane
Toronto ON M5S 3J4
Canada

416 979 2217
800 367 6360

mail@chbooks.com
www.chbooks.com